10⁵⁵

THE FOREST WORLD

THE FOREST WORLD

The Ecology of the Temperate Woodlands

Eric Duffey

A & W Publishers, Inc.
New York

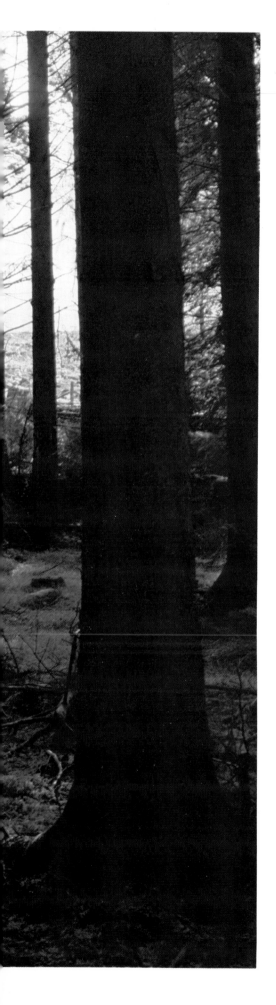

CONTENTS

INTRODUCTION   7

THE MAKING OF THE FOREST   13

    Forest zonation in the northern hemisphere   16
    Temperate forests of the southern hemisphere   39

THE FOREST AS A LIVING WORLD   45

    Insects: the foliage feeders   50
    Forest birds   65
    Mammals of the forest   79

THE FOREST TODAY   103

    First steps in forest protection   104
    Felling the giants   106
    Lichens: pollution indicators   108
    National parks as sanctuaries   112

    Acknowledgments   118
    Index   119

First published in the United States of
America in 1980 by A & W Publishers, Inc
95 Madison Avenue
New York, New York 10016
By arrangement with Orbis Publishing
Limited

Library of Congress Catalog Card
Number: 79-91274
ISBN: 0-89479-060-9
Printed in Italy

INTRODUCTION

About a third of the land surface of the world is forest covered. This is a generous estimate since it includes types of savanna and scrubland where trees may be few or scattered. Originally, before man challenged the dominance of forests, probably twice this area was tree covered and today the process of decline continues as the human population expands and increases its demand on the land. This process is virtually complete in Europe where natural forest survives only as small relics in the mountains. Elsewhere in less developed countries it is proceeding at a rapid rate wherever climatic conditions are suitable for human settlement. Although so much natural forest has disappeared, man is still very dependent on timber to satisfy his needs. The most efficient way of achieving this is to create commercial plantations of fast-growing trees or to modify existing forest that only the most useful species are retained.

For a long period of his history, man had an ambivalent attitude to the forest; although it provided food, shelter, warmth and essential materials, at the same time he destroyed it as if it were an enemy. Perhaps part of the reason was that human beings were not originally forest animals and were seldom at home in the forest environment. There are of course tribes in some parts of the tropics who have learned in the course of human evolution to adapt to forest ways but the dominant people who occupied the earth as we know it today originated from more open lands, their attitude being to fell the trees and put the land to some other use. Fear of the forest is written into a great deal of our recorded history and still seems to be a deeply ingrained aspect of human nature.

There are of course good reasons why a social animal such as man would find it difficult to live in a forest world. Forests are great storehouses of carbohydrates, in particular cellulose – the main constituent of timber – but not much accessible protein is produced. This is because ground-feeding animals, including the domestic stock of early man, depend on the herb layer and the leaves of trees and bushes for their food supply. In general this is scarce and of low quality compared with what is available in more open lands. Yet man was undoubtedly deeply impressed by the grandeur of the ancient forest, a fact reflected in the reverence for trees which forms part of many religious beliefs all over the world. In India trees were considered to be the abode of the souls of the dead so when a man was thought to be tormented by demons the villagers would hold a ceremony to provide a tree where the evil spirit could dwell peacefully without molesting the patient. In ancient

Left: The largest known conifer – giant sequoias in Yosemite National Park, California.

Below: Splendid beech trees in the Mark Ash Wood of England's New Forest.

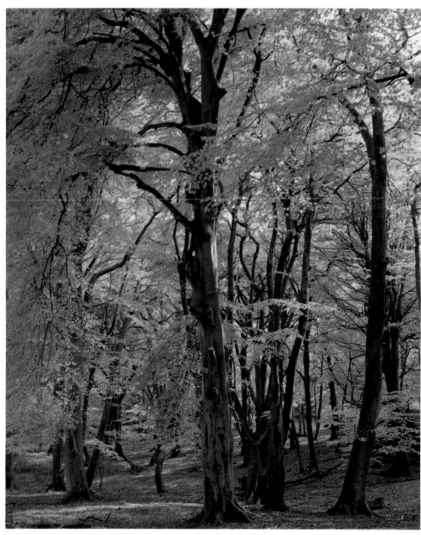

Greece it was often customary to make a sacrifice to a deity before cutting down trees for timber. In the Homeric hymn to Aphrodite it is said that the tree nymph is wounded if the tree is injured and dies when the tree falls or is cut down.

Although trees played an important part in the religion and life of primitive man, there was little he could do to destroy the giant species such as the Californian redwood, even if he wished to, because his tools were completely inadequate. Where trees did not attain such a great size they were not immune to the attentions of early man, for example in Neolithic times in various parts of Europe. During the period 3000 to 5000 years ago, fire was used to clear the forest in order to open up areas for grazing animals, or for primitive cultivation which was just beginning to develop. And extensive deforestation took place even earlier than this in the Middle East. This proved to be disastrous in low rainfall areas because erosion and desiccation rapidly created desert conditions which have survived to the present day. We know that vegetation previously existed because the remains of human settlements, irrigation channels and reservoirs have survived, although today they are covered by drifting sands and the land is bare of trees. Today, in Israel and countries bordering the Sahara desert, reafforestation schemes using a collection of dew and underground water supplies, are conquering the desert wastes.

Forest history

The events which followed after primitive man cleared the forest during the Neolithic period have been traced by examination of the pollen in certain types of soil, usually bog peat, where it is preserved. Over a long period of time the pollen accumulates within the ever-deepening peat layer. These deposits, throughout the peat profile, can be dated, showing that the amount of tree pollen began to decline some 4000 to 5000 years ago in Europe, with a corresponding sharp increase in the pollen of herbaceous plants, cereals and agricultural weeds. In Denmark, where some exciting studies have been made on the history of the old forest of Draved, the occurrence of weeds characteristic of open areas was followed by the appearance of new tree species such as willow, aspen and birch. The presence of birch strongly suggests that man used fire to help clear the forest, because on fertile soil it is only after burning that this tree replaces a mixed oak forest. Provided there is no further clearing, the vegetation gradually changes until the forest takes over once more. All this evidence seems to suggest that man cleared the original forest with axes, burned the cut material and then planted small fields of cereals and used areas for pasturing grazing animals. These were probably only temporary and evidence suggests that some lasted scarcely more than fifty years.

In the Breckland area of eastern England extensive

Below: Enjoying the forest shade, a group of red deer, a species found throughout temperate Europe and Asia and introduced into North America, Australia and New Zealand.

flint mines which are thought to date from about 4000 years ago are known in an area called Grimes Graves. Archaeologists believe that much of the flint was used to make axe heads for forest clearance on the light, sandy soils. The 540 identified pitshafts indicate a considerable demand for flint tools and that mining activity extended over a very long period. Some of the flint tools were exported to other parts of the country but much of the material seems to have been used locally. Although for centuries the sandy soils of Breckland seemed to be capable of supporting only a poor open heath hardly worth cultivating, they are thought to have been covered with an open oak forest in Neolithic times where clearings could easily be made for cultivation. The evidence for a forested landscape is derived from animal remains and the type of tools used in the pits for excavating the flint, of which the most common was the antler of the red deer, expertly used as a pick. Other bone remains include the extinct wild ox known as the auroch, the roe deer and wild pigs. All these animals occur in forest or open forest conditions, so they indicate to us the type of landscape in which Neolithic man lived.

The deforestation was probably carried out by the 'slash and burn' technique, the trees being felled with a flint or stone axe and the wood burned to provide a layer of ash which for a short time would provide a fertile bed for the germination of cereals.

Although the land would have been abandoned when it was no longer capable of growing useful crops, regeneration of trees may have been prevented by domestic grazing animals. It is known, for example, that sheep grazed the Breckland heathlands in Roman times and continued to be of major importance until the twentieth century.

European woodland history since the Middle Ages has been the subject of some interesting recent studies. For example, Hayley Wood near Cambridge, England, is described in a series of documents beginning in 1251 but it almost certainly existed much earlier than this. Some of the most reliable evidence for tracing woodland history can be derived from the vegetation, earthworks and other surface features which we can actually see on the ground as we walk under the trees. No ploughing takes place in woodlands and there is very little disturbance to the soil, so that the historic record is preserved as long as the woodland remains. Hayley Wood, like most ancient woods, is surrounded by a broad bank and a ditch, with the former on the wood side. This seems to have been a common arrangement, since the earthwork was intended to make it easier to construct a fence around the wood and also to drain the adjoining land. The bank gave the wood a permanent boundary which was marked in detail on the earliest large-scale maps, showing even small irregularities in shape.

A characteristic of the earliest forest boundaries is that they are not straight or uniformly curving but tend to be sinuous or slightly meandering, a construction which probably dates from the original forest clearance when the boundary had to be taken round large individual trees. Another feature of a primeval wood which can be seen at Hayley is the presence of irregular hollows where water collects in wet seasons, often up to a few inches deep. It is possible that natural irregularities, particularly on the clay soils of West Cambridgeshire, date from the end of the last glaciation. If the area had been ploughed in the past these depressions would have been destroyed. This supports the view that Hayley Wood has been in existence with the same boundaries for at least 720 years.

Its survival for more than seven centuries is clear evidence of its value to the local community. It is known that it produced a variety of different timber products. The smaller trees and bushes, known as the coppice, were cut every few years and then allowed to grow again, so that successive crops of poles or underwood were obtained. The larger trees, called the standards, which were scattered among the coppice, were allowed to reach full height and then felled to yield timber plus a certain amount of firewood from the branches. In this way the wood maintained a regular yield of material yet retained its forest character and value from generation to generation.

Unfortunately coppice-with-standards management has become rare because it is labour-intensive and there is no longer a market for such timber. This traditional management regime is perpetuated in some British woodland reserves today because it is important for the maintenance of certain plants and animals. In the spring after coppicing, sunlight streams in through the open canopy and plants such as the oxlip, bluebell, wood anemone and species of violets grow much more vigorously. By the third season coppice regrowth is producing a good deal of shade and these plants decline in vigour, while shade-loving species such as dog's mercury begin to thrive again. Neglect of coppice management would disrupt this cycle of flowering and also affect the insects and other animals associated with these plants.

Although Neolithic man was widely dispersed throughout western Europe, the process of deforestation was slow. Nevertheless it continued for over 3000 years and by the early Middle Ages some parts of Europe were deforested almost to the same extent as they are today. In North America, on the other hand, the native populations had little impact on the enormous forest areas and it was not until the seventeenth century, when the flow of European immigrants began to increase, that extensive forest destruction began accelerating greatly during the course of the nineteenth century.

Exploitation on a grand scale

At that time most of the Indian tribes were hunters rather than cultivators. The forest was an essential part of the environment and protected the game on which they depended for food, clothing and other essentials of life. But most of the European colonists in North America came from farming communities with a tradition of cultivation; in order to survive they had to rely on the only way they knew to make a living, ploughing and cultivating. To do this the forest had to be destroyed.

When the European immigrants reached the vast prairies of the Mid-West they found ideal conditions for farming settlements, but some biologists believe that even these endless rolling grasslands might have been forest covered in the distant past. The evidence is the presence of islands of forest in the prairie region and the fact that if trees are planted they seem to grow quite well without irrigation. It seems possible that before European man brought the horse to North America, the plains Indian, hunting on foot, helped to keep the prairies open, when they hunted buffalo and the prong-horned antelope, by using fire to drive the game into areas where they could be more easily captured.

The timber wealth of North America was so great that in the early days of colonization by the European no one believed it could ever be exhausted and no thought was given to the future. In the states of Michigan, Minnesota and Wisconsin, for example, enormous forests of softwoods were felled, particularly during the last half of the nineteenth century. The object was maximum profit in the shortest possible time with the result that the slash – that is the unwanted branches – was left on the ground and created a severe fire hazard. Very extensive and destructive fires often burned for weeks because there was no organized fire-fighting service. Further north in Canada, exploitation of the forests was not as extensive and came very much later because the hard winters and the more difficult terrain made the land less attractive for farming.

The great speed of forest clearance in North America is shown by an example in New England, where from between 1620 and the second half of the nineteenth century about 40 per cent of the land surface was cleared for agriculture. The most extensive and earliest was in the three states to the south, New Hampshire, Vermont and the southern third of Maine. Even if the land was not wanted for agriculture it was cut over for timber and pulp and then much of it subsequently burned. We can say with certainty, therefore, that all the pre-colonial forest has long since gone from these states and only isolated fragments exist further to the north. Though great was the devastation, North America was the first country to establish National Parks – Yellowstone in north-western Wyoming being established in 1872.

Right: Trees festooned with moss on Queen Charlotte Island off the coast of British Columbia.

THE MAKING OF THE FOREST

Trees are ancient plants and there is a rich fossil record in certain types of sedimentary rocks. In Oregon, North America, fossil remains have been found in deposits which are 54 million years old and it has been possible to identify the swamp cypress, black oak, hickory, sycamore, various species of maples, the dawn redwood, the maidenhair tree, box elder, and elm. All of these trees can be found growing in different parts of the world today, although several are no longer found in North America and two, the dawn redwood and the maidenhair tree, are natives of central China and are not known to grow anywhere else in the world. These fossil trees were found in deposits laid down during what is known as the Eocene period when the climate was much warmer. For example, in Alaska, plants lived to within eight degrees of the North Pole and included such well-known temperate trees as the walnut, where today there is only a frozen treeless waste.

The first tree-like plants were recorded at a much earlier period towards the upper Devonian period, 380 million years ago. The earliest seed-bearing plants were recorded millions of years earlier but the arboreal growth form did not develop until the evolution of secondary tissues known as xylem, which formed an additional layer each year and so strengthened the main stem. Several types of tree-like plants have been recorded in which annual growth shows up in section as a narrow band of small cells and then larger ones. This suggests that although climatic conditions were favourable there was an alternation of seasons and climatic conditions were not uniform throughout the year. Some of the best-known fossil plants showing this feature are *Aneurophyton*, *Tetraxylopteris* and *Archaeopteris*. The last of these was a tree reaching over one hundred feet in height, a measurement calculated from the tapering of stumps which have been found as fossil specimens. By the middle Devonian, when this species appeared to be common, there was also evidence that side branches were being produced to give a more treelike form. It seems likely that if *Archaeopteris* was common at that time in the course

of evolution, the first forests appeared over the land surface of the world. These early trees produced minute spores rather than seeds and it was not until the second half of the Devonian period that the first true seed appeared. This was a female gametophyte in which there was a store of food material to sustain the young plant after germination and give it an opportunity to become established.

The 50-million-year Devonian period was succeeded by the lush vegetation of the low-lying swamplands of the Carboniferous. This was a time of tall trees, evolving in some cases almost into giants, and it is to this abundance of swamp forest that we owe our present coal deposits. Coal was formed by

Left: The deciduous cypresses or Taxodium *species are natives of the southern parts of North America and Mexico. Below: The Petrified Forest National Park, Arizona has the largest and most colourful deposit of petrified wood in the world. These fossil trees date back to the Upper Triassic period, 160–170 million years ago.*

much earlier in the fossil record. The arborescer habit evolved during the late Devonian and reache its peak during the Carboniferous period. *Lepidoder dron*, for instance, grew to a height of 27 m c more and one has been recorded as 35 m hig] These giant lycopods appeared to have decline rapidly during the end of the Palaeozoic era.

During the Carboniferous there were also sever groups of seed plants known collectively as gymnc sperms; one of these was the conifers. They ha small leaves which were spirally arranged but wer nevertheless reminiscent of those found in man trees living today. The reproductive organs wer borne on separate male and female cones and th wood structure was closely comparable to that c modern conifers. The conifers expanded during th Permian era and increased still further during th Mesozoic but in the Cretaceous period some of thes primitive trees began to decline. Another group c gymnosperms that arose in the Carboniferous wer the cycads which also became reduced in th Cretaceous though several species live today in th tropics and sub-tropics. The ginko group of gymnc sperms is even further reduced at the present day t one species, *Ginko biloba*, the maidenhair tre though in the Mesozoic this group was very divers Few ginkos survive in their native China but the have been planted extensively in other countries.

Above: The fossil tree Walchia was one of the early conifers and first appeared in the Upper Carboniferous period. Its structure is similar to the living genus Araucaria.

the gentle fluctuations of the earth's surface, which alternately raised and lowered the land, resulting in exposure or submergence of the forests. During submergence the lush vegetation was rapidly covered by sediments, compressed, and ultimately converted into coal. This cycle was repeated many times during the Carboniferous period and produced the vertically layered seams of coal which we know today. One of the best-known trees of the Carboniferous period was *Lepidodendron*, a treelike form of the simpler club mosses which appeared

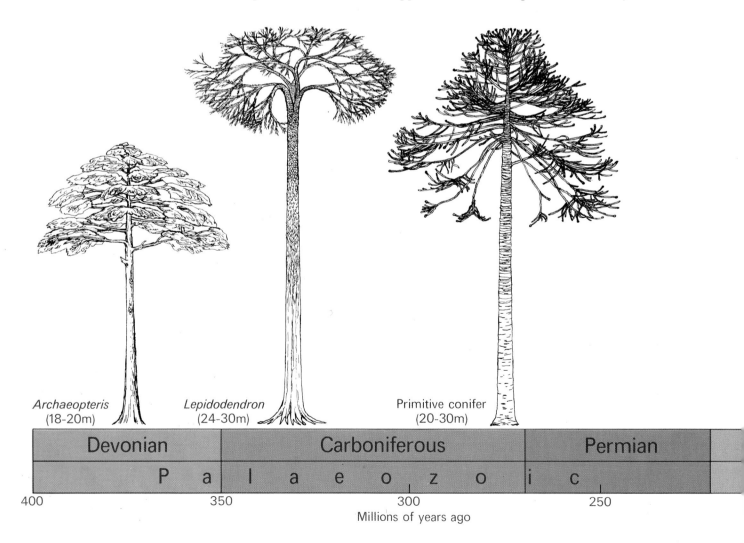

Archaeopteris
(18-20m)

Lepidodendron
(24-30m)

Primitive conifer
(20-30m)

Devonian	Carboniferous	Permian	
P a l a e o z o i c			

400   350   300   250

Millions of years ago

During the early Cretaceous the first of the flowering plants began to appear and by the late Cretaceous they were the dominant type of vegetation.

The modern forest

By the time man had evolved as a primitive primate, enormous areas of forest existed throughout the world and a glance at a map of the potential forest regions will show that almost all the north temperate zone below the cold of the arctic wastes was capable of growing trees. The limiting factors were only water supply – at least ten inches of annual rainfall are needed – and summer temperatures high enough for growth to take place even though the season may be quite short. In the Euroasian land mass we find that approximately 45 degrees North is the beginning of temperate deciduous forests and the northern limit of the steppes and evergreen woodlands. At about 55 degrees North the deciduous forests give way to the northern boreal forests of conifers, which themselves extend to about 65 degrees, when they give way to the tundras of the arctic region.

The temperate climatic zone, which has a marked but not too prolonged cold season, is well developed only in the northern hemisphere. Apart from certain mountainous districts in the southern Andes, Tasmania and in New Zealand, it is absent from the southern hemisphere. Deciduous trees which are so characteristic of the temperate zone shed their leaves in the autumn as an adaptation to the cold season. It is not facultative but obligatory, occurring even if the trees are grown in a greenhouse where they are protected from freezing temperatures. The factor responsible for the change in colour of the leaves in the autumn, even before the first frosts occur, is still unknown. It is possible that it is associated with decreasing day length as the converse of this is known to determine the onset of the breeding season in many animals.

A few temperate forest trees retain their leaves throughout the year and show a special sort of environmental adaptation. For example, holly is Atlantic in its distribution and ivy subatlantic, so that both species avoid the eastern continental regions where there are severe winters. The same is true for gorse and the common broom, while two other woody species which retain their leaves, the alpenrose and the cranberry, survive the cold but only beneath a protective covering of snow. The loss of the thin deciduous leaves in the winter and the protection of the buds from water losses represents a saving of material when compared with the action of freezing on thick evergreen leaves. Nevertheless the new leaves formed in the spring must have a sufficiently long warm summer period of at least four months to produce enough organic material for growth and for the maturation of the lignified axial organs. They must also form reserves of nutrients which will be needed for the fruits and buds of the following year.

There is a loss of water from the twigs of deciduous trees even during the winter, the extent of which varies from species to species. For example, the central European beech avoids the severe cold of the east European winter, although the oak extends as far as the Urals. When we reach the continental regions of Siberia the only broadleaved deciduous trees are species of birch, the aspen and the mountain ash. In the boreal regions of the Eurasian continent, where the summers are too cool and too short for deciduous trees, we find that evergreen conifers become dominant. Their needle-shaped leaves are more resistant to cold in the winter and when the warmer weather returns in the spring they are capable of starting up photosynthesis immediately so that the short growing season is more effectively exploited. The average deciduous tree requires a warm season of at least 120 days with a mean daily temperature of 10°C, while some conifers manage with only 30 days. Unlike the tropics the deciduous forests of the temperate regions of the northern hemisphere contain relatively few species and in

Cycad
(2-7m)

Ginkgo
(15-30m)

Magnolia
(9-15m)

	Jurassic			Cretaceous			Caenozoic
M	e	s	o	z	o	i	c

150   100   50   0

Millions of years ago   Present day

some cases single species dominate over considerable areas. One of the most widespread trees in western Europe is the beech, which is found in the montane regions of the Pyrenees and the Alps, in the Bosnian mountains and in the Mediterranean wherever there is a cloud belt.

FOREST ZONATION IN THE NORTHERN HEMISPHERE

The boreal coniferous forest zone of the northern hemisphere, with its cold to temperate climate, encircles the entire globe through northern Eurasia and North America. There is no sharp boundary between deciduous forest and coniferous forest. The transitional area usually has mixed stands of a few coniferous species and a few deciduous species, or else a mosaic-like arrangement with pure deciduous forest where there is a more fertile soil and pure coniferous forests in less favourable habitats with poor soils. In East and North America different species of *Pinus* represent the conifers in the mixed stands. In the neighbourhood of the Great Lakes it is mainly *Pinus strobus*, Weymouth Pine, although *Tsuga canadensis*, Eastern Hemlock, and *Juniperus virginiana*, Pencil Cedar, are also found. Pine trees are often the pioneer woody species following forest fires or when arable land is abandoned. In Europe the situation is rather simpler. On the poor glacial sands extending in wide belts in central and eastern Europe, pure pine forests occur, and some of these are in regions which belong climatically to the decid-uous forest zone. These woodlands are called bor, while on the rather better loamy soils where there is

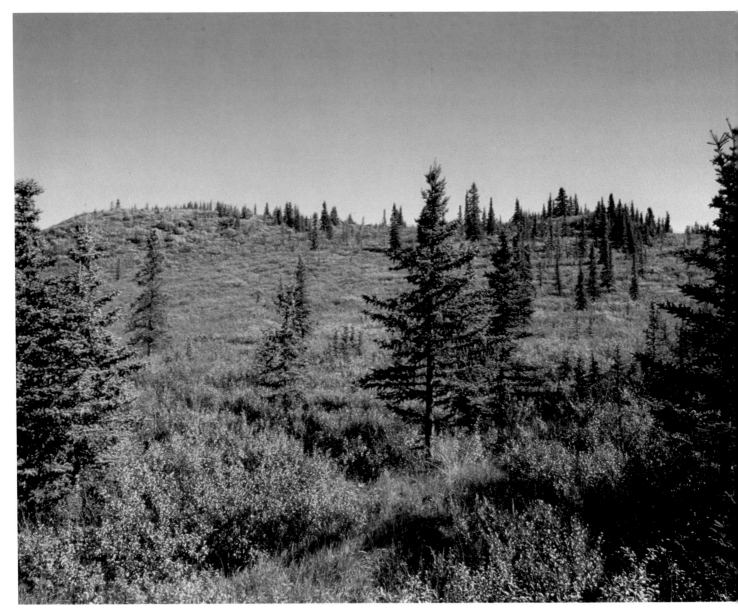

an additional tree stratum of oak, the forest is then called subor. On more fertile soils hornbeam occurs and finally on loess there are the zonal deciduous forests known as grud, with oak in the upper stratum and hornbeam in the lower.

These forests have been drastically altered by human interference. Forest fires and felling of deciduous trees for fuel have encouraged the growth of pines, whereas, elsewhere, the removal of pines for use as building material has resulted in the formation of pure deciduous forest. In southern Scandinavia, and central Eastern Europe, spruce and oak are common. They occur in the same geographical region but tend not to mix, usually one or the other species being found depending on the soil type.

The northern boundary between the boreal zone and the tundra is where there are only about thirty days with a daily mean temperature above 10 degrees Centigrade and where the cold season lasts about eight months. The climate varies from place to place and in extreme cases a yearly temperature range of 100°C may be registered. This is from a maximum of +30°C in the hottest part of the summer to a minimum of −70°C in the coldest part of the winter.

As with the deciduous forest, the coniferous forests of North America and those in eastern Asia contain a large number of different species, whereas those in the Eurosiberian region contain very few. In the latter case only spruce, *Picea abies*, and the pine *Pinus sylvestris* are of any real importance in the European boreal zone. In the eastern regions of Siberia, however, *Picea abies* gives way to *Picea obavata* while a number of other species also occur in the forests. The proportion of spruce decreases until in the continental parts of eastern Siberia it is entirely absent. At the same time the common larch is replaced by another species, which is very widespread in Siberia. As we go further to the east into China and Japan, and the nearby parts of eastern Asia, the number of coniferous species increases greatly.

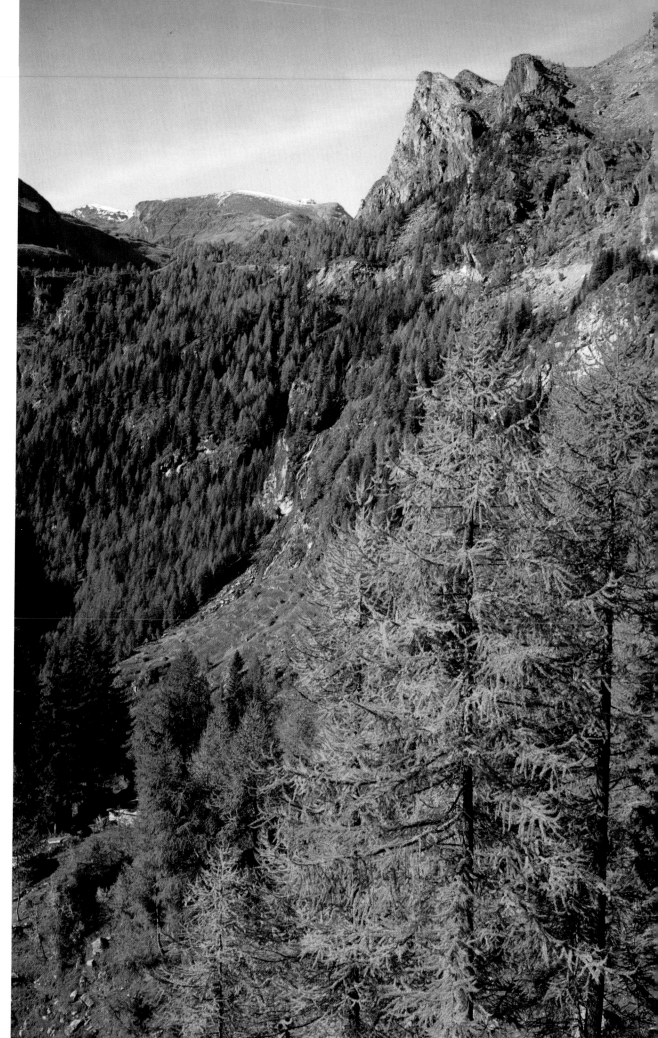

Left: Start of the tundra – in the Yukon the long cold winter and frozen soil below the surface even in summer prevent the establishment of true forest.

Right: Some of the finest forests of European larch are in the Italian alps shown by this scene of the Val d' Aosta close to the Gran Paradiso National Park.

Forests of Europe and northern Asia

The most important forested region in the world is undoubtedly the USSR. The total forested area is 832 million hectares, and this is greater than that found on any other continent, including North America. Nearly 1500 species of trees and shrubs grow in the USSR and many are of great importance to the national economy. Nevertheless some seventy-eight per cent of all forests are coniferous and this reflects the continental climate over most of the territory. Probably the commonest tree in the Soviet Union is the larch, which covers 274 million hectares and accounts for more than forty per cent of all the Soviet forests. And among the deciduous species the most common is the birch, which accounts for 13.5 per cent of the total forest area. Other important trees are the pine, spruce, fir, cedar and the dwarf mountain pine and among the deciduous species the most important next to the birch are the oak, beech, aspen, alder and lime. Nearer the tundra zone, dwarf species of birch and willow predominate, together with cowberry, bushy alder and cranberry.

Below: An aerial view of the Mackenzie river, Canada, which flows from the Great Slave Lake north to the Arctic Ocean. Here it passes through northern forests near the limit of tree growth.

■ Mountain vegetation		■ Mixed forest, mid-latitudes	
■ Tundra		■ Broadleaf forest	
■ Northern coniferous forest		■ Mediterranean scrub	
■ Conifer forest		□ Steppe	

The taiga

The true northern forest zone forms a wide belt stretching across the Asiatic continent from European Russia to eastern Siberia. The occurrence of this woodland depends very much on the climatic characteristics of the regions and is not confined to particular latitudes. In certain areas it penetrates as far north as the Taymyr peninsula, reaching 72° 30N. Its widest zone is in eastern Siberia, where it extends from 49°N to 72°N, that is more than 2,300 km from north to south. These forests are usually called the taiga and consist of pine, spruce, fir, larch and cedar. There are many scattered lakes and extensive marshy areas. Cold winters with very low temperatures are recorded but the short summers may be warm, with July means of 10 to 20°C. The late spring and early autumn frosts which are not unusual prevent the growth of broadleaved trees. The Karelian taiga which borders the White Sea coast has forest which are dominated by pine and spruce in which cowberry and bilberry are also very common. Growth is slow so that the wood tends to be very compact and fine-grained. In the same area there is also a birch known as the Karelian birch, whose wood has a knotty texture and is in great demand for furniture and other types of woodwork. The fauna of this forest is much richer than that further north, including some fifty-five species of mammals and nearly two hundred species of birds. Interesting species include sable, Asiatic chipmunk, northern pika, hazel hen and Siberian jay.

Because of the great area covered by the taiga it is divided by foresters into subzones. The middle taiga is of great economic importance because conditions are more favourable for tree growth and consequently the forest is intensively exploited. In the south the southern taiga has a milder climate with considerable amounts of rain, and the growing season may be from 150 to 160 days. Other trees begin to appear, particularly the aspen, with alder in certain places, and occasionally elm and lime. In the west Siberian taiga, for example in the region of the River Yenisei, the landscape consists of hilly plateaus with narrow steep-sided canyons. The forests consist mainly of Siberian spruce, cedar and fir towards the southern parts of this region. In the

north there are spruce, cedar, larch and birch, and in the west the characteristic tree is the larch, with some spruce and pine. The height of all trees in open areas may reach five to six metres, but where they are sheltered from the cold winds the larch forests are denser and the trees reach twelve to fifteen metres in height. In the eastern parts of Siberia the forest is called the Yakut taiga, and in area covers more than one and a half million square kilometres. Winter temperatures in this region may fall to −65°C and the annual mean may be no higher than −12°C. These forests are dominated by the Daurian larch, with a mixture of pine, birch and aspen. Spruce seldom occurs and cedar is only found in the south, while the fir is unknown.

Another form of mountain taiga forest is found in the mountain ranges near Lake Baikal and further to the east. The mean annual temperatures are −6 to −7°C and the maximum range may be as high as 93°C, while the growing season is from 85 to 120 days. In the northern part there is a continuous mountain taiga of larch, occupying the lower zones, while from 1300 to 1500 metres there are thickets of the Japanese stone pine. In other areas one encounters the Jeddo spruce and the Asian white birch. This extensive taiga penetrates far to the south, where alternating with steppe country it extends into the

People's Republic of Mongolia before giving way to the main zone of steppe landscape.

Sakhalin Island has its own form of mountain taiga. This is rather surprising because the island is situated in a relatively southern latitude with the fiftieth parallel going through its mid-section. Nevertheless it has a harsh climate. Summers last only two to two and a half months and the snow carpet may persist for seven months of the year. The very great length of the island from north to south gives it southern flora characteristics derived from North Japan and Manchuria, while in the north the flora is closer to that of eastern Siberia. The forests on the lower slopes are mainly Jeddo spruce and the Sakhalin fir with Erman's birch higher up the mountain slopes. On the western ranges in the south of the island this birch forms extensive forests, often with dense and generally impenetrable thickets of the Kuril bamboo. On the northern slopes exposed to the cold winds of the sea of Okhotsk and on the plains of northern Sakhalin are forests of Daurian larch and Japanese stone pine. Above the stone pine there is a belt of high mountain vegetation in which the Pontic azalea is a typical representative.

Although the taiga forest zone suffers a severe climate and the human population is low, it is a region of considerable economic importance because of its size – more than 600 million hectares – and because it accounts for approximately eighty per cent of all Soviet forests.

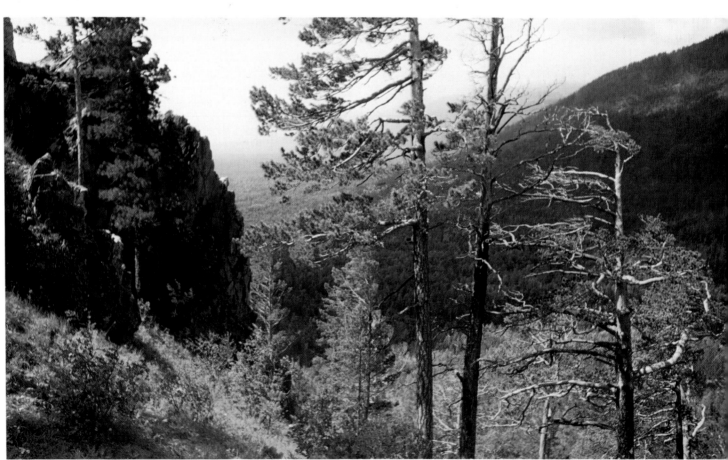

The mixed forest belt

To the south of the taiga extends a belt of mixed coniferous and broadleaved forests, characteristic of the European part of the Soviet Union and of the Far East, where milder climates prevail, but absent from the vast expanses of Siberia.

Due to Atlantic and Pacific Ocean influences the winters are not too severe nor the summers too hot, and the rainfall is sufficient for growth. The European type of mixed forest belt is characterized by spruce, Scots pine, pedunculate oak and the small-leaved lime. Various species of maples are also present, together with shrubs such as hazel and spindle.

In the Far East the mixed forest forms a rather narrow belt in maritime territory where climatic conditions are milder and more humid, so allowing many more species to flourish. For instance, in the Ussuri forests as many as 150 species have been recorded, including some relicts from the Tertiary period, such as the acutifoliate yew, the Amur cork tree, Manchurian walnut, and Chinese magnolia vine. The most productive of these forests grow on mountain slopes from 200 to 300 m above sea level, where lianas and epiphytes make them look rather like subtropical forests, although there are no other features in common. The trees consist of a first storey of Korean cedar or Manchurian fir, while the second and third storeys include broadleaved species, Magnolian oak, Amur lime, Manchurian lime, various maples, Manchurian walnut, Amur cork tree, elm and a species of birch. The shrubby layer is interesting because it includes hazel, wild jasmine, wild pepper, barbery, the Amur grape, the magnolia vine and a type of seedless grape called the kishmish. Ginseng, a plant used as a cure-all by by the Chinese, and now popular in the West, is also found in this mixed type of forest.

Broadleaved woodlands and forest steppes

To the south of the mixed forests are the broadleaved woodlands of the USSR. In the European part of the country they cover a relatively restricted area, extending as a narrow belt from the Carpathians to the Ural mountains. The soils are fertile, creating an area where there is extensive agriculture and a dense population. The most important forests have the pedunculate oak, the European ash, the Norway maple, various elms, the small-leaved lime, pear and apple. In the west the hornbeam and the beech are two typical trees. Oak is also one of the common species in the far-eastern broadleaved forests, but generally grows on less fertile soils. The broadleaved forest zone merges to the south into open steppe country but a transitional zone is recognized as a type of forest steppe forming a narrow continuous belt from the foothills of the Carpathians in the west of the USSR to the Altai, the Salair ridge and Kuznetsk Alatau mountains.

There are three regions of forest steppe, the eastern European, the west Siberian and the Daurian-Mongolian. The first is characterized by broad-leaved forests of oak and hornbeam, or oak, ash and lime. In the west Siberian region the climate is more continental with hot summers and cold winters but the principal species is birch and not oak. The Daurian-Mongolian forest steppe is less extensive, occurring chiefly in the foothill areas of Transbaikalia, where one finds stands of Daurian larch and pine with a considerable admixture of birch.

The clearly marked forest belts which have been described for the USSR and still exist in a relatively natural form in this enormous land mass break down to some extent in Europe, where so much of the forest has been cleared or modified by man. Most of the fertile soils have been largely reclaimed for agriculture to serve the needs of the growing population, leaving only patches of the original forest.

Above left: Taiga forest near Irkutsk in Siberia – many of the trees are bent over by the weight of snow.

Left: Siberian taiga forest in the Sayan mountains which extend from the Yenisei river to the USSR-Mongolia border.

Above: Mixed evergreen forest in the Central Japanese Alps – a mountain region of modest height consisting of some recently active volcanoes.

Western Europe

Although natural forest is virtually absent from the densely populated and highly industrialized countries of western Europe, timber production is an important aspect of the economy. In Britain and the Netherlands, the forested areas do not amount to more than seven or eight per cent of the land surface, but elsewhere, in France, Germany, Spain, Italy, for example, about a quarter of each country consists of woodland. In Scandinavia, particularly Norway, Sweden and Finland, the proportion of forest land may reach fifty-five per cent. Much of the commercial woodland grows on the poorer soils where timber production is more profitable than agriculture. These include mountains, steep slopes in river valleys, sandy soils such as Les Landes in France, Breckland in England, or western Jutland in Denmark. In coastal areas forests of maritime pine fulfil an important function of stabilizing dunes and preventing wind erosion. Some timber may also be taken by selective felling and in southwest France the production of resin, collected by making cuts in the bark, is an important local occupation.

Other forest products are also important in many countries. Around the shores of the Mediterranean both in Europe and North Africa the cork oak produces its valuable crop of bark every twelve to fifteen years. The sweet chestnut and the walnut produce nuts of commercial value while the acorns from the different species of oak are important for wild boar, deer, and other forest animals. Many fungi are sought by local people in the late summer and autumn, both in pine and deciduous forests. One of the most valuable is the group known as truffles. They grow hidden in the soil and vary in size from smaller than a walnut to the size of a fist. The white truffle is highly valued as a spice and grows in leaf-mould in deciduous and coniferous woods. The most prized species is the black truffle, which is largely confined to southern European forests and forms its fruit body during the winter.

In Europe one of the most important functions of the forest is to provide game for the hunter. Apart from deer and wild boar, which are the principal game species, pheasants, blackcock and capercaillie are much sought after. In some countries only a few birds may be shot and most wild birds are protected unless, like the wood pigeon, they are regarded as pests. In other countries where the law is weak because hunters form a strong political lobby, many more bird species are killed. Italy and France have more hunters than any other European country – about one million permit holders in the former and two million in the latter. In both countries each hunter has about thirty hectares of land – the lowest in Europe. The income from the licences is used partly to maintain a series of hunting reserves which act as 'sanctuaries' for wildlife for at least part of the year.

Far left: A spruce forest in central Sweden. As the old trees fall, the canopy opens up allowing more light to penetrate the forest floor and new young trees to develop.

Above: The Landes forest of south-west France is one of the largest areas of conifers in Europe. The wide fire-break emphasizes the constant danger of fire.

Left: The wild boar is one of the most sought-after game animals of European forests. It is still very widespread and extends into Asia; it often does much damage to crops including vineyards.

25

Remnant forests of the Mediterranean

The European forest plant communities may be classified in four different groups. Starting with the Mediterranean area there are the lowland and hill forests with evergreen oaks and pine trees, the scrub communities called matorral, the deciduous forest with oak and chestnut and the montane forest of beech, pines and silver fir. The first of these – the lowland and hill forests dominated by evergreen oak – are potentially the climax communities in the Mediterranean region, but this type of forest is seldom seen in its mature state because man has had a devastating effect on it. Many areas have been cleared for agriculture and the remainder have been so modified by intensive cutting, grazing and burning that they seldom look like a forest area at all. It seems likely that forests of the holm, or evergreen, oak at one time probably covered two-thirds of the Iberian peninsula, and associated with it one would expect *Viburnum*, *Arbutus* (the strawberry tree), and many woody climbers. In parts of Portugal and southern Spain where there is a fairly low rainfall a closely related species of oak called *Quercus rotundifolia* takes the place of holm oak.

There are still a few examples of the holm oak

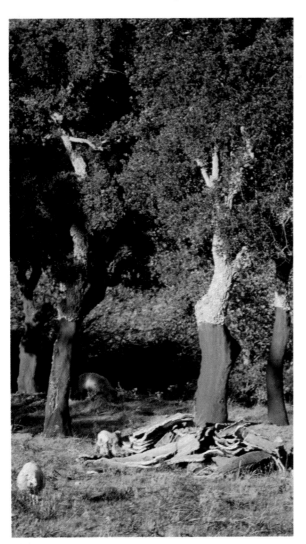

forest in the Catalan hills but most of it is reduced to a sort of thicket with scattered trees and an abundance of the kermes oak, which invades when the original forest cover is destroyed. Along the French Mediterranean coast the holm oak forest is virtually non-existent except on the island of Port-Cros. This is now a National Park and a remnant of the type of Mediterranean forest which was formerly very widespread throughout Provence and along that part of the Mediterranean coast east of the Rhône. On Port-Cros the trees are not very large but they give some idea of what the original forest was like. Their thick evergreen leaves screen the bright Mediterranean sun from the ground surface and give the impression of deep shade and a rather sombre atmosphere, in which there is not very much insect or bird life – although in the later part of the summer the song of the cicadas is everywhere to be heard.

Generally, however, the destruction of the Mediterranean forest has been so extensive that its original form is largely theoretical. A much more characteristic feature of the landscape is provided by what is known as the maquis, a type of scrubby vegetation which has replaced the original forest. As man gradually destroyed the forest with fire and grazing animals, maquis became established over enormous areas. In some places it looks like a stunted woodland dotted with conifers and a few oaks, while in others it is an immense shrubbery or tangled thicket with a considerable number of different species of woody evergreen bushes.

Presumably the original forest would re-establish itself if allowed to do so, but this rarely happens: as the shrub growth becomes denser, so it is burnt off again to provide better grazing and to enable grazing animals to penetrate to the few herbaceous plants and grasses. The evergreen maquis vegetation is usually defined as a formation reaching a height of somewhere between two and four metres, and may be so dense that it is difficult to force a way through. Closely allied to this is another Mediterranean type called the garigue, which is more or less an open community of small shrubs about knee-high and with very aromatic foliage. There are gradations of every type between these two and the term matorral is usually taken to include both. Matorral formations are particularly widespread on shallow soils and in low rainfall areas with high evaporation. They are typical of the sunny hills of the south and the stony plateau in the centre of the Iberian peninsula. One distinctive type includes the dwarf palm, which is often very abundant and the only species of palm native to Europe.

The cork oak, which is a native species of Mediterranean Europe, is grown extensively in Portugal and provides one-third of the world's cork supply. The tree is also grown in southwest Spain, in Catalonia in eastern Spain and in North Africa. The cork oak woods that one sees today are open and often

Below left: Collecting cork is still a valuable crop in the Mediterranean even in this age of plastic bottle stoppers.

park-like forests. Formerly they were much more widespread, but many of today's productive woodlands have been developed on land previously covered by matorral and of very little value to the local people.

The olive is another important tree in the Iberian peninsula and in Italy. In the former it is not a true native, although it has been under cultivation for at least two thousand years.

Three pine trees are of special importance in the Mediterranean region of Europe. The Aleppo pine is very widespread and forms open forests on shallow denuded soils, particularly on limestone. It is well developed on the dry coastal hills and is the tree which gives the wooded appearance to much of the Mediterranean coastal landscape not yet spoiled by development. The maritime pine dominates the more humid coastal hills, particularly on acid soils and on sand, but in the last fifty years or so the faster-growing eucalyptus has replaced it and is now quite widespread in parts of Spain and Portugal. The umbrella pine has a rather limited dis-

Below: A terraced hillside with olive trees; a nylon net helps collect the rich olive harvest.

tribution in the southwest of Spain, particularly in the Coto Doñana, and in southern France in the Camargue region. It has a distinctive umbrella-shaped canopy and produces a large and nutritious seed.

In the hills where the climate is cooler and more humid, and the rainfall between 700 and 900 mm, the semi-evergreen Lusitanian oak replaces the holm oak and forms extensive forests along the western Atlantic hills and also in the southwest of Spain. A good example of this forest is in the Mondego valley of central Portugal. The white oak is another species which forms an open climax forest in the hills of the Mediterranean region, where the temperatures are not too high. In the Cantabrian mountains it occupies the transitional zone between the pedunculate oak and the beech forests, while in the Pyrenees it is found between the Lusitanian oak forests and the beech. With it are the lime and the Montpellier maple, and an associated flora rich in species.

The deciduous Pyrenean oak is a characteristic forest species of the central sierras and Iberian mountains at altitudes of between 1200 and 1400 m. The pedunculate oak, if it is undisturbed by man, often occurs with the Pyrenean oak and the sessile oak. Another common species in this type of deciduous forest is the sweet chestnut, which often combines with oak to form well-developed forests in the Cantabrian mountains, particularly in the National Park of Covadonga.

The montane forests of France and the Iberian peninsula are dominated by the beech. It is the most common mountain tree in the Cantabrian mountains, the Pyrenees and the Massif Central, with a wide altitude range from about 600 to 1900 m. It often forms very dense and uniform forests, particularly on steep valley sides where it is not so easily exploited by man. Other trees growing with the beech include the ash, elm, sycamore and the evergreen species box and yew. In general the beech favours the warmer, south-facing slopes of the mountains, but in the Cantabrians on the dry stony southern slopes it is replaced by the Spanish juniper and the holm oak.

In Italy there is a great range of woodland types due to the striking differences in climate and temperature according to the greater or lesser proximity of the mountains. For example, the greater part of Tuscany and adjacent provinces as far as Rome enjoy a mild winter climate which is suitable for olives as well as vines, but it is not until south of Terracina that the true luxuriance of the vegetation of southern Italy develops. The lowlands, especially on the Tyrrhenian shore, have many olive, orange and lemon orchards, as well as date-palms and other trees. In the hilly districts, but not far from the shore, there are forests of oaks and chestnut, and higher still we find firs and pines. Some of the finest forest areas in Italy are in the Apennine mountain range, especially the Abruzzo National Park. This is an area of nearly 30,000 hectares and probably the best known national park in Europe. It has one of the most spectacular of the Apennine landscapes, with the highest point reaching 2247 m. It includes the Sangro valley, which has an undulating glacial relief with cirques and stretches of moraine interspersed by faults and karstic phenomena. The upland forests to the timber line are dominated by beech, with some of the finest woods of this species in Europe. A number of other trees are found with the beech, particularly birch and yew. Lower in the valleys there are forests of hornbeam and turkey oak and locally the close relative of the hornbeam, the hop-hornbeam, with the flowering ash. In one or two areas there are forests of the downy oak, together with the sessile oak, which is a much more widespread species throughout Europe.

In contrast the alpine park of Gran Paradiso has few of these southern species, the most common being the larch, spruce and pine. The silver fir and the mountain pine are rather local, and because of the high altitude there are few deciduous trees. The park was originally a royal hunting reserve created by King Victor Emanuel II in 1856. In spite of an attempt to preserve the game, all the large predators

Left: The Gran Sasso d'Italia mountains and the wide valley of the Campo Imperatore in the central Apennines. The scattered beech forests become much more extensive further south.

Right: The Covadonga National Park in northern Spain is a very beautiful area but extensive grazing by goats, sheep, cattle and horses has greatly reduced the forested area.

subsequently became extinct, notably the bear, wolf, lynx, and also the bearded vulture, the last being shot in 1912. Immediately after the First World War King Victor Emanuel III handed over the shooting rights and his properties in the Gran Paradiso to the Italian state so that it could be made into a National Park. During the Second World War it suffered a great deal of damage by illegal hunting, and the ibex was reduced to a few hundreds. Further south, however, in the magnificent beech forest of the Abruzzi region of the Apennines, the wolf and the brown bear have managed to hang on. How long they will survive is difficult to say, particularly in the case of the wolf, which is not protected outside the national park area.

Some of the most widespread and characteristic Mediterranean trees penetrate into North Africa but are confined to the narrow strip of land between the Atlas mountains and the Mediterranean Sea. One of the most frequent is the Montpellier maple, which extends from Spain to Asia Minor and also along the North African shore. The Aleppo pine is another very characteristic Mediterranean tree which is confined to the Mediterranean shores of Europe and North Africa, and generally occupies a fairly narrow maritime belt. On the other hand the so-called maritime pine only occurs in the Mediterranean zone from Spain to Italy, including the Pyrenees and reaches only a small part of North Africa on the

African side of the Straits of Gibraltar. Another very typical Mediterranean tree is the stone pine, which extends from the Atlantic coast of Spain to the eastern shores of the Mediterranean and includes the Black Sea, although it is not known on the African continent. All these trees have their uses for building, furniture, and other types of woodwork; the Aleppo pine, which is widespread in the Holy Land, is said to have supplied the wood for the cross on which Jesus Christ was crucified.

Some Mediterranean trees are equally well known outside the region because of their magnificent shape and great size. The best example is the cedar. There are two species, the cedar of Lebanon, and the Atlas or Algerian cedar in North Africa. Although they are natives of hot dry countries, they grow well much further north in Europe and are both popular trees in parks and botanic gardens. However, in their native lands they are mountain trees, particularly in the mid-Atlas region of Morocco. The cedar forests were formerly much more extensive and there is some evidence that their clearance began as far back as Roman times. The Atlas mountains, which stretch from Morocco through Algeria into Tunisia, have a flora with many European characteristics. The dominant species of trees are oaks and conifers while the cork oak makes up the great forest of Mamora. The evergreen oak and other *Quercus* species together with juniper are also wide-

Below: The magnificent cedar of Lebanon, well known in Europe and North America as an ornamental tree, has virtually disappeared from its native country. The photograph shows one of these last remaining stands surrounded by arid, treeless country.

spread. In Tunisia, out of two thousand species of plants which have been recorded, about three-quarters also occur in Italy. The cork oak is a common forest tree with the Aleppo pine, wild olive and the evergreen oak. In most Mediterranean countries man's activities have had a devastating effect on the forests for thousands of years and many forest plants have disappeared. The woods were cleared for cultivation and, of course, unrestricted grazing by sheep and goats has prevented the growth of young trees. In Greece, which has one of the richest floras of any country in Europe, the destruction caused by the goat is said to be incalculable. Greek biologists fear that unless drastic measures are taken to control indiscriminate grazing the destruction of the greater part of the wild vegetation of Greece will become inevitable in a few scores of years. The remarkable recovery the vegetation can make when grazing is controlled has been shown in the region of Mount Athos. An ancient monastic law does not allow female animals to be kept so there are no flocks of sheep, goats or cattle. The result is that the condition of the wild vegetation there is immeasurably better than in any other district of Greece.

In the area of another monastery some fine reafforestation work is being conducted by the Athens Society of the Friends of the Trees, again by preventing grazing. On Mount Pindus there is a nature reserve of some 4500 hectares which has a landscape of outstanding beauty. As well as a fine fauna which includes the brown bear, wild cat, roe deer and boar, the forests are some of the best in Greece, although they are not adequately protected from cutting and grazing animals. The forest includes beech, different species of pine, plus outstanding specimens of the horse chestnut, limes and numerous other trees. The World Wildlife Fund has supported the reafforestation work on Mount Pindus for several years.

Below: The Pindus group of mountains in Greece has fine forests of pine and beech. The area also boasts an outstanding flora, and wildlife – including the brown bear.

Above: Avalanche damage is a constant danger where there are steep slopes and a heavy snowfall, as in the Mount Rainier National Park of Washington's Cascade Mountains.

Eastern Europe

Although natural forests are so rare in western Europe and the Mediterranean region, some remnants still survive in central Europe. One of the best examples is the Bialowieza National Park in Poland, which covers 4716 hectares and is a strict reserve in the central part of an extensive forest complex which bears the same name. It is situated in a flat plain of Pleistocene sands and loams with a range of beautifully preserved deciduous forests of lime and hornbeam, with alder in damper areas, but elsewhere mixed deciduous and coniferous forests of pine and oak. There are many bogs, swamps and open waters throughout this forest area. Until the

sixteenth century it was visited only by hunters s the vegetation remained nearly intact. During th latter part of this century the first villages wer established around the edge of the forest and in th seventeenth century more permanent settlement were created by clearing glades inside the wood land. This was followed by the building of road cutting of timber and cultivation. A good dea remained relatively untouched, however, becaus from 1888 to 1914 the forest was managed as a hunt ing ground for the Tzars. A certain amount c damage was caused to the vegetation by excessiv game populations until a reserve was created afte the First World War. In 1932 the area became

National Park. Bialowieza is an exceptional wild-life reserve, apart from its herd of bison it has beaver, lynx and an extremely rich avifauna.

On the Czechoslovak/Polish borders there is another splendid forest National Park, in the Tatra mountains. The whole area forms one unit with 1,546 hectares in Poland and 50,000 hectares in Czechoslovakia. The Tatra massif is composed of granites and limestones with extensive montane forests of beech and pine up to 1800 m where there is a scrubby mountain pine zone before the alpine pastures are reached.

In the fourteenth century the Tatra forests became a royal hunting preserve but the gradual increase in human settlements was accompanied by extensive clearance, grazing by sheep and cattle and burning of the mountain pine to extend the pastures. The number of sheep increased to about 40,000 during the Second World War, resulting in forest destruction and increased soil erosion. By 1960, however, the numbers had fallen to about 8000 and the present management objective is to reduce them still further to ensure full recovery of the forest structure.

The forest suffered in other ways from the sixteenth to nineteenth centuries. In 1502 silver and copper ores were discovered and foundries built to exploit them. A rapid expansion of this activity took place when new deposits including iron ore were found in the eighteenth century. Foundries need a great deal of wood as fuel and by the early 1800s large areas of forest had disappeared. Some forest stands were completely cleared and caused the extermination of the beech-fir in the lower forest zone. Later this area was planted with spruce and these artificial forests persist to the present day.

Natural disasters occur from time to time in all forests and in mountain areas many trees are destroyed or damaged by storms, snowfalls and avalanches. In the Tatra region a fierce wind known as the 'halny' sometimes sweeps over the area. In 1898 62,000 trees were blown down, in 1925 80,000 were destroyed and further damage occurred in 1947 and 1968. Avalanches are not so destructive nowadays because of more intelligent forest management, but at the end of the nineteenth century and the beginning of the twentieth they were much more frequent because grazing and burning had destroyed the upper protective zone of mountain pine.

Today the Tatra forests serve the community in a different way, as a National Park – a natural laboratory for biological studies and educational work as well as attracting large numbers of tourists who come to enjoy the scenery and mountain air. Zakopane, in the foothills of the Polish Tatras, is a thriving holiday town and a focal point for climbers and hikers. The same type of development is found on the Czechoslovak side at Tatranská Lomnica, where a fine new laboratory has been built for park studies.

Below: Although tree cover is the best protection against avalanches reaching the lower slopes, trees may sometimes be destroyed by heavy snow falls. Here, in the French Alps trees have been broken off by an avalanche of the previous winter.

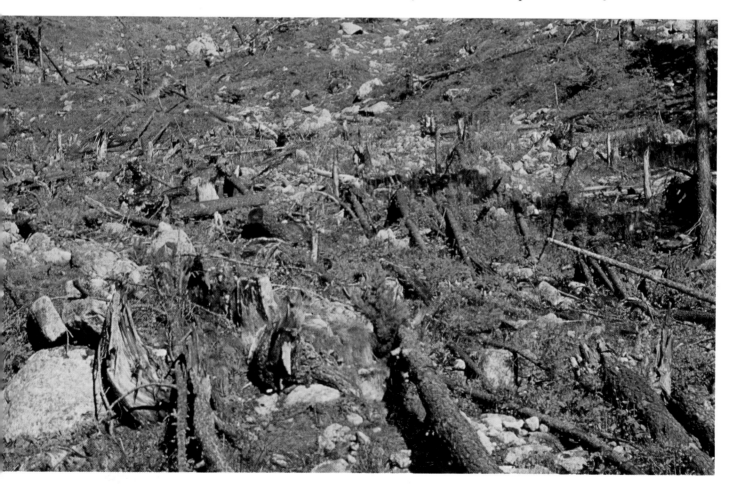

North America

The evergreen shrub community described for the Mediterranean region under the general term 'matorral' has its counterpart in North America – the 'chaparral'. There are three types; the first in California where the winters are wet and the summers dry and the vegetation is dominated by scrub oaks and chamise; secondly the inland chaparral of Arizona and New Mexico dominated by the Gambel oak and thirdly the Great Basin sagebrush, much of which has been converted to rangeland for cattle.

For the most part these plant communities are highly inflammable and for centuries fires, started by man or by lightning, have swept through the chaparral, clearing away the old growth and making way for the new. The grass and fresh shoots are excellent food for deer, sheep and cattle, but after a while the new shoots mature, the shrub canopy gradually closes up, the dry litter accumulates and the conditions are ideal for another fire.

In the southeastern parts of the United States of America along the Gulf Coast and in the hammocks of the Florida Everglades and the Keys is a type of temperate evergreen forest, restricted to a region of warm maritime climate and characterized by oaks, magnolias, gumbo limbo, palms and bromalids. The southern tip of the Florida peninsula has been of special importance to the naturalist since the establishment of the unique Everglades National Park in 1947. The Park extends over more than 5280 sq km of marsh and forest fed by rivers draining from the north. Unfortunately more and more water – the 'life-blood' of the wildlife communities – is being diverted or used for industrial development and urban needs.

The plant life is of six principal types, with the unusual names of hammocks, bayheads, cypress heads, pinelands, mangrove swamps and marsh. The hammocks are small islands raised a few inches above the marsh and support a jungle-like growth of broadleaved hardwoods, mosses, ferns and epiphytes. On some the tall, graceful royal palm grows; the only place in North America where it is a native. On others a few remaining Madeira mahoganies can still be found, the largest having been felled during logging activities before the creation of the Park. Bayheads are dense with cypress, red bay, magnolia and holly, often interlaced with vines. The pinelands are interspersed with hardwoods and palms, while in the coastal areas are the dense tangled growths of

■ Mountain vegetation	▨ Mixed forest, mid-latitudes
▨ Tundra	▨ Broadleaf forest
▨ Northern coniferous forest	▨ Mediterranean scrub
▨ Conifer forest	▨ Steppe

Right: The Sierra Nevada of California is best known for its giant sequoia – here is different aspect, the autumn colour of its deciduous trees.

red, white and black mangroves.

The temperate deciduous forest is best developed in eastern North America. Several different types intergrade one into another. In the north is the hemlock/white pine/northern hardwoods forest, which occupies southern Canada, the northern USA and along the Appalachians to North Carolina and Tennessee. White pine used to be the most characteristic species but extensive logging in the past has reduced it to a subsidiary role. This forest is rich in tree species, the most common being beech, sugar maple, yellow birch, black cherry and oak. In southern Indiana, central Minnesota and east to western New York are forests dominated by sugar maple and beech and from Wisconsin and Minnesota to northern Missouri is a similar forest in which basswood is co-dominant with sugar maple. Further south is another type of temperate deciduous forest, said to be one of the most magnificent in the world, very rich in species with the yellow poplar dominant.

In the northern USA, through Canada to the tundra, there is a broad belt of northern coniferous forest which penetrates south to Mexico along the Rockies and Sierras of the Coastal Mountain Range. The most typical trees are the eastern hemlock, jack pine, red pine, white pine and white cedar. The composition of tree species varies from place to place depending on climate and soil type but in general the northern coniferous forest occupies a glacial

Left: The Muskoka region of Northern Ontario is a region of forest and lakes, very popular with the Canadians in the summer.

Below: Tall straight trunks of western hemlock and Douglas fir in the Cascade Mountains of Oregon.

landscape with cold lakes, bogs and rivers and is reproduced in similar form throughout the boreal regions of the old world as well as the new.

South of Alaska along the Pacific coastal range is a very distinctive type of temperate rain forest. As the moisture-laden winds move inland from the Pacific Ocean they deposit a high rainfall on the western-facing mountain slopes. During the summer the cool sea air brings in heavy fog which collects on the tree foliage and drips to the ground, adding more moisture. These conditions support a lush forest vegetation of western hemlock, western red cedar, sitka spruce and douglas fir. Further south, in California, where the annual rainfall diminishes but is still high, the famous sequoia forests survive, although only small areas remain where the lumberjack has not been active. Some of these trees – great wonders of nature reach 91 m and are over three thousand years old. The sequoias rise in clean, red columns among firs and sugar pines and disappear upwards above the canopy of lesser trees. The tallest of the sequoias, *Sequoiadendron giganteum*, include famous individual trees like 'General Sherman' and 'General Grant', both about 82 m. This species was introduced to Europe in the mid-

nineteenth century and is now common, although the tallest there does not exceed about 49 m.

At a high elevation in the Rockies where the winters are long and the snowfall heavy, is a sub-alpine coniferous forest characterized by the Engelmann spruce, alpine fir, white-barked and bristlecone pines. At lower elevations the douglas fir and ponderosa pine become more common. In these regions the rainfall is much less than along the western slopes of the coastal ranges but nevertheless has a significant effect on forest ecology, depending on local conditions of aspect, soil and elevation. Magnificent examples of these forests can be seen in the National Parks of the Pacific and mountain States.

TEMPERATE FORESTS OF THE SOUTHERN HEMISPHERE

The great difference in the proportion of sea to land between the southern and northern hemispheres has fundamental effects on the origin and distribution of forest zones. In the north we have seen that belts of the same forest type have a circumpolar distribution because of the great land masses and small area of sea. In the south it is a different problem; the land areas are small, ancient and separated by great oceans. However, in spite of this, Charles Darwin and Joseph Hooker found surprising similarities between the forests of South America and New Zealand, and this was studied in greater detail by later botanists. Fossil trees have also been discovered in parts of Antarctica where trees can no longer grow because of the severe climate. There seems no doubt that formerly a great antarctic continent existed, enjoying a pleasant climate and covered with vegetation. From this area certain genera of plants and animals penetrated into New Zealand, Tasmania and the southern part of South America and have survived, while elsewhere a great ice sheet covered the continent. If we view the world from the South Pole it is clear that the temperate zone consists largely of great oceans in contrast to the equivalent latitudes in the Northern Hemisphere, where there are the great land masses of Eurasia and North America.

There is one very noticeable difference between the forests of southern Chile and those of the northern hemisphere: the former are preponderantly of evergreen trees and have few conifers because in the maritime climate there is a fairly constant temperature throughout the year. This is related to the fact that the temperate zones in the South American continent lies between 45° and 55°S, whereas in the northern hemisphere it is mainly from 55° to 65°.

There are two types of forest in southern Chile which are of special interest to the biologist. The first is the Valdivian Forest, named after the Chilean town of Valdivia on the Pacific coast and which clothes the slopes of the Andes on both east and west sides. This forest forms a vigorous growth averaging

Left: A fallen redwood giant surrounded by living trees. Redwoods are confined to the coastal mountain ranges of northern California.

Below: The lodgepole pine is one of the most important timber trees of North America, it has been introduced to many places in Europe.

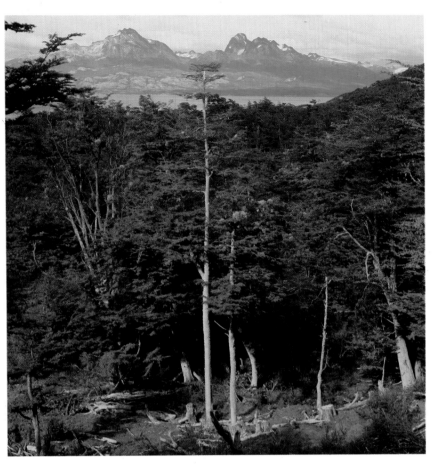

New Zealand

The temperate range of the southern beeches is well illustrated by their distribution in New Zealand because the northern tip of North Island has a climate which is almost subtropical while the southern part of South Island is cool temperate. If we follow this route from north to south, four main forest associations can be identified. First there are the mixed hardwoods, consisting of kauri, podocarp woodlands, secondly the podocarp mixed hardwoods, thirdly podocarp and beech forests, and finally the southern beech woodlands. Each is characterized by different tree associations. The kauri, which is a splendid tree growing to a great height and occurring sometimes in dense stands, is a member of the conifer family Araucariaceae. The young trees have a reddish bark which becomes grey as they get older, and which sloughs off in large scales. It is believed to be a very long-lived tree and certainly there are specimens which were alive 2000 years ago. When the colonists first came to New Zealand in the last century, many of these giants were probably in stately middle age. These magnificent trees were soon chopped down for their tough durable wood and also for their rich gum, used for making lacquers and varnishes. Today, only remnants of kauri forest survive on the North Island.

The canopy of the kauri is often festooned with

forty metres in height and consisting principally of trees with persistent leaves of the magnolia and laurel type. The very many species of the myrtle family, a vast group of aromatic trees and shrubs, give the Valdivian forest a pleasant fragrance. The ground flora is striking because it includes the biggest moss known anywhere in the world and many other species which form a loose thick carpet beneath the trees. The tree trunks, especially those species with a scaly or fibrous bark, are covered with creepers, lianas and epiphytes. The soil is always damp and has a thick humus layer with abundant leaf litter, fallen twigs and branches.

Further south the Valdivian forest is less rich in species of plants and animals and at about the forty-eighth parallel it gives way to another type known as the Magellanic forest, so called because it extends down to the Magellan Straits and the storm-swept Tierra del Fuego. Only six species of trees extend as far south as the Straits, three of them southern beeches of the genus *Nothofagus*. These trees provide some of the best evidence of the previous existence of an antarctic continent free from ice. They are only known in the southern hemisphere with eleven species in South America, five in New Zealand, three in Australia, five in New Caledonia and about twenty in New Guinea. This distribution shows that although it is a characteristic genus of the southern temperate region it also extends into the subtropical zone.

Above: The southern beech Nothofagus *reaches as far south as Tierra del Fuego the southernmost part of South America.*

Right: A view of Papakari Creek, Westland, New Zealand, tree ferns amongst podocarp forest.

Far right: Warm temperate rain forest with tree ferns in the Westland National Park of New Zealand. This park situated in the foothills of the southern Alps, has many lakes, rivers and glaciers as well as subtropical rain forest.

Above: The genus Hebe *includes about 130 species nearly all confined to New Zealand and Australia.*

large quantities of epiphytic vegetation growing on the branches, perhaps fifty metres above the ground. Each tree is dioecious, that is it has male and female flowers and when the green cones are ripe they fall to the earth, breaking open to liberate the winged seeds. The other dominant trees, the podocarps, are tall softwood trees with small curved pointed leaves rather similar to the yew. Two well-known species have the Maori names of Totara and Miro. The former has reddish bark which peels off in strips and greenish fruits which attract many birds. The bark of the Miro is similar to that of the kauri and its fruit is like a small purple plum. All the podocarp trees are of particular importance to the New Zealand timber industry but they grow in a mixed hardwood forest with a number of other species which are not valuable as timber. These include species with the picturesque Maori names of Taraire, Towai and the Kohekohe. The last of these may reach a height of fifteen metres and as it grows, its glossy leaves change from a yellowish colour to dark green. It has long spikes of small yellow flowers which are borne below the leaf canopy directly on the trunk and give rise to bunches of fruits containing scarlet, flesh-covered seeds.

This brief description of one of the main types of New Zealand forest refers to the north part of the North Island and because of exploitation during the last century, something like 400,000 hectares is all that remains of the once vast kauri forest. Further south we find a second type of forest, the podocarp mixed hardwood forest typical of the lowland areas in the North Island, having dominant trees known as Rimu and Rata. These curious trees belong to the myrtle family and have thick evergreen leaves. The northern Rata grows to about thirty metres, an epiphyte which may develop as a seedling in the angle of another tree's branches. As it grows its roots gradually surround the host tree, which eventually is completely smothered. The epiphyte is not parasitic and uses the host tree as a support, not as a source of nourishment.

There are a number of hardwood species associated with the podocarps, some of which belong to the laurel family and form trees up to about twenty-five metres. The Kamahi, which is common in the northern forest associations, is a tall spreading grey-barked tree with leaves dark green above and lighter below. It has creamy pink flowers and the stalks point upwards to bear red seed capsules. Sometimes these are so profuse that the whole tree acquires a rich warm hue. The podocarp/beech forests are characteristic of the colder climates. They are generally found further south in New Zealand and in the foothills and middle altitudes.

Away from the swampy ground beech species of the genus *Nothofagus* begin to appear in the podocarp forest, forming a dense canopy. The black and hard beeches are not found in the extreme south, whereas the mountain, red and silver beeches can thrive in harsher, more exposed mountain lands and so penetrate into the colder latitudes. These splendid trees are very distinctive and can be easily recognized: the red beech has a fluted trunk with a dark red bark, whereas the hard beech is almost black and the silver beech greyish white. The best way of distinguishing these five species is not by their trunks, however, but by their leaves, as each has a characteristic shape and size.

The mountain beech is the hardiest of all the New Zealand trees, with a considerable climatic range. It thrives in areas where there is an extremely high rainfall, harsh frosts and gale-force winds. The mountain beech frequently forms the timberline with gnarled stunted trees, which finally give way to tussock grassland. Silver beech is widely distributed at high altitudes throughout New Zealand and is often dominant in Southland and sub-dominant to the red beech in North Westland. The red beech is the most common species in the north-east of Southland and can also survive a fairly rigorous climate.

During the second half of the nineteenth century enormous areas of forest were cleared to meet the demand for farmland and consequently a great deal of useful timber was wasted. New Zealand did not have a Forest Service until 1919 but well before then exotic trees were being planted to replace the native forests as they were cleared. The most popular was *Pinus radiata*, the Monterey pine, from California. By 1968 the native forests in New Zealand covered less than a third of the area which was tree-covered when the Europeans first settled the country.

The commercial forest area totals rather less than 300,000 hectares, while amenity and biological forest reserves cover about 55,000 hectares. Within both are a number of protection forests on very steep slopes which cannot be felled without serious

Above: Nothofagus beech forest in South Island, New Zealand. These beautiful native forests are fast disappearing as commercial forestry takes over.

consequences of erosion. On the west coast about five per cent of the lowland forest is to be protected as 'biological' reserves and a similar amount in the Southland region. However, some biologists consider that such provision is insufficient because so little indigenous forest below 600 m survives on North Island and this may also happen to the South Island. Commercial forestry affects many other parts of the environment, particularly the waterways, which can be polluted by toxic effluents produced during the processing of the wood. A number of chemicals occur in timber, particularly in the heartwood. These can give rise to problems during the processing and may be sticky materials like resins in conifers, chemically active like tannins in some eucalypts and in red beech, or else dark colours which cause difficulties in the manufacture of white paper. These unwanted materials have to be removed in the pulping process by solution and then disposed of.

Exotic timbers such as *Pinus radiata* are usually treated with preservatives to fight fungal attack and prevent discolouration. These chemicals are copper-chrome-arsenate, boron salts, sodium pentachlorophenate or a mixture of fluoride and arsenate may be used. The excess solution runs off the timber and

these extremely toxic substances often escape into the environment. In 1971 the New Zealand forest products mill produced 610 tonnes of pulp and paper and used 91 million litres of water per day. It is reused three times before being returned to the local river system with its suspended wood fibre, clay, titanium oxide, lime, lignin, sodium sulphate and other organic compounds and chemicals. Some of these can be removed but a significant proportion reaches the natural drainage system.

These types of problems occur wherever timber production and paper-making are important local industries and New Zealand is only cited as an example. In Sweden, where a number of the timber-processing plants are situated by inland lakes, poisons in the effluent were taken up by invertebrate animals and plants and then by fish and eventually found their way into fish-eating birds such as the osprey. Although lethal doses were rare, these chemicals interfered with the breeding behaviour and the survival of the young causing the population of these birds to fall dramatically. Measures are now taken to minimize effluent discharge and the osprey is fortunately recovering. We can only hope that this more enlightened attitude will enable a better balance to be established between nature and man everywhere.

43

THE FOREST
AS A LIVING WORLD

No one can look at a large tree such as an ancient oak, a lofty beech, or venerable yew without being aware of the remarkable complexity of its structure: the massive trunk with its furrowed bark bearing its own flora of mosses and lichens; the buttressed base creating dark crevices where small animals may hide; the intricate pattern of bough, smaller branch, twig, bud and leaf with flowers and fruit according to season. The shade cast by the canopy and the spreading roots seeking nourishment in the surface soil greatly influence the vegetation of the forest floor and this, in turn, affects the animal life. Another important facet of this complex tree world may not be so obvious: all old trees are dead in parts, branches die through insect or fungal attack, the tree may be damaged by high winds and lightning and in some cases the whole of the heart-wood may have rotted away, leaving the tree hollow but nevertheless still alive. In the primeval forest undisturbed by Man there is more dead wood than living, much still on the tree but even more on the forest floor. This is fully utilized by a rich insect fauna including some of our most magnificent species, as well as by fungi, algae and other primitive plants like mosses and liverworts.

This complex of living organisms and the non-living environment together form what the ecologist calls the *ecosystem*. All the plants and animals and the material on which they live are inseparably interrelated. That is, they depend on each other or else are affected in some way by the activities and processes taking place in other parts of the environment. The total system displayed by one tree is so complicated that it is far from being fully understood by the scientist – who has even more difficulty when trying to explain the way in which many trees live together to form the forest.

Almost any species of tree would serve as an example to examine more closely the different components of the forest ecosystem, but let us take the familiar oak tree, which is so widespread throughout the northern hemisphere. The genus is a large one and includes about 450 species. The Iberian peninsula has twelve and there are fifteen in the Balkans,

but by far the greatest concentration is in Mexico, which has about 125 endemic species and a further 75 which extend into North America or south into Colombia. Oaks are also abundant throughout Asia, reaching southern China, Japan and other parts of the Far East.

There are two native species in Britain, *Quercus robur* and *Q. petraea*, and they have dominated the forests in lowland regions for thousands of years partly because they grow very readily on many different types of soils and partly because they provided so many of Man's needs that they have been preserved and planted during centuries of woodland

Far left: A plantation of Scots pine in Norfolk, England – in older woods more light is able to penetrate the canopy allowing a ground flora to develop.

Left: In Northern Europe oak trees take at least twenty years before they flower – the flowers are tiny and are produced on catkins during the month of May.

The life of the beech

Beech forests are the most common type of forest found in temperate Europe. They are found scattered through the hills and lower slopes of mountains in central and southern Europe and extensive forests still survive in the lowlands of France and Germany despite extensive clearance. In Britain the remaining pockets of beech woods are confined to the southern counties.

A well grown beech tree casts a dense shade in summer and deposits a heavy layer of leaves during the autumn. The root system of a beech is also particularly well developed and lies near the surface. These conditions do not favour a rich ground cover. One group of plants that thrive in the dense shade are the birdsnest orchids which lack the green plant pigment chlorophyl and obtain their nourishment directly from decaying leaf litter. These orchids are yellowish-brown and are named from the round and tangled root system. Other orchids to be found are the common helleborine, white helleborine and the narrow-leaved helleborine. In young and mixed woods where the canopy is not so dense, one can find bluebells and wood sorrel, wood anemone and yellow archangel depending on the soil, if it is alkaline or neutral.

At ground level a beech wood lacks a buzzing insect life but higher up in the canopy there is a good assortment of insects including the beech aphis which sucks the juices from the leaves and can cause much damage. Over fifty species of the larger moths have been recorded feeding on beech including the lobster moth, vapourer, grey dagger and marveille de jour. The caterpillar of the lobster moth has a bizarre threat display in which it rears up on the front part of its body vibrating its long thin legs and at the same time bending over its swollen rear end. It can further defend itself by squirting out a jet of formic acid which is enough to stop any bird predator from snapping it up. The magnificent longhorn beetle *Rosalia alpina* is found in mature beech woods of central and southern Europe where there is a good supply of rotten timber on which its larva feeds. This beetle shows an interesting expansion of its range northwards into southern Sweden though it is still absent from Britain.

The wood warbler is the bird one associates with beech woods. It does not seem to mind the normal lack of ground cover, relying for its food on the abundance of defoliating insects of the canopy. An interesting resident of montane beech woods is the middle spotted woodpecker which seems to confine itself to deciduous forests more than its relatives. It is constantly on the move, examining all dead wood for insect food. The collared flycatcher, a hole nester and the woodchat shrikes are also birds that favour beech woods

especially those growing on mountainsides. In the autumn the beech mast provides welcome food for migrant birds from northern Europe including chaffinches, bramblings and hawfinches.

The beech marten is an adaptable predator although not as arboreal in its habits as the related pine marten, it preys on rodents and ground nesting birds. The garden dormouse is an attractive rodent; its name is misleading as it prefers mature deciduous woodland although it can be found raiding fruit trees in large gardens and orchards. An unusual feature of this animal is its ability to shed its long tufted tail when attacked by a predator. The fat or edible dormouse feeds mainly on nuts, beech mast in particular, and in Britain where it has been introduced it is found particularly in the Chiltern hills where fine beech woods still survive. The brown bear, more than any other large mammal, has suffered from the deforestation that has occurred of the larger beech forests, one of its main natural habitats.

1 *Pipistrelle bat*
2 *Song thrush*
3 *Eagle owl*
4 *Red squirrel*
5 *Middle spotted woodpecker*
6 *Jay*
7 *Collared flycatcher*
8 *Garden dormouse*
9 *Edible dormouse*
10 *Beech marten*
11 *Nuthatch*
12 *Woodchat shrike*
13 *Brown bear*
14 *Common shrew*
15 *Wild cat*
16 *Yellow-necked mouse*
17 *Weasel*
18 *Hedgehog*
19 *Badger*
20 *Roe deer*
21 *Longhorn beetle (Rosalia alpina)*
22 *Wood warbler*
23 *Sparrowhawk*
24 *Lobster moth*

management. Throughout Europe the oak was regarded with special affection because it grows to a large size, providing acorns for feeding animals and tannin for preserving leather, while its timber is of great strength and durability; it also splits easily for construction work and coppices freely to supply an abundance of sticks and stakes.

The history of the oak in Britain can be traced back through the last 10,000 years, mainly from fossilized remains such as pieces of timber, twigs, charcoal, bud scales, leaves, fruit and cuppules frequently found preserved in peat deposits of various kinds. Oaks occur abundantly in buried forests, that is those trees killed at some time in the past and hich have gradually become covered with peat, which accumulates during very wet conditions. These are usually called bog oaks, and are often stained almost black by the reaction of iron in the ground water with tannins in the wood, and when dry are exceedingly tough. The oaks that were embedded by the sea as it encroached over the Fenland basin died about four thousand five hundred years ago, in the Neolithic period, and even in these subfossil trees we find traces of the fauna associated with them. These consist mainly of galleries made by boring beetles or larvae, but occasionally the insects themselves are found. A farmer splitting bog oaks for firewood, near the fenland town of Ramsey in Cambridgeshire, found large galleries which contained two perfect specimens of the splendid longhorn beetle *Cerambyx cerdo*. This species is still widespread in continental Europe and known as an insect of ancient forest, but is extinct in Britain. The tree trunk in which these two specimens were found was a large one, more than 12 m long, and the timber was dated by the carbon-14 method to be about 3690 years old.

Since that time the oak fauna has probably not changed very much and the insect species which have disappeared from various parts of Europe have been lost mainly because man has destroyed their forest habitat. Nevertheless entomologists are agreed that the oak has one of the richest insect faunas of any tree and this is particularly so in northern Europe where the number of native tree species is not high. In general, native trees have richer faunas than introduced ones because their invertebrate life has evolved over a long period of time. When a tree is moved from its native environment to another country it is usually transported as seed so that it grows in its new home without any of the insect life which is adapted to live on it. An example in Britain is the sycamore, which was taken there in the sixteenth century and although it has gradually acquired a fauna, this is not nearly as rich as that found on oak.

Another possible reason for the difference between the oak and the sycamore is that the former is generally associated with the richer fauna of warmer climates, whereas the latter belongs to a genus of trees exclusive to the cool temperate regions which have a much poorer fauna.

Below: The larva of this handsome longhorn beetle (Cerambyx cerdo) feeds in the wood of oak and fruit trees.

49

INSECTS: THE FOLIAGE FEEDERS

When the oak acorn germinates and the first leaves appear, the young tree is vulnerable to damage by grazing animals, particularly rabbits, deer and small rodents. If the growing point is eaten off, development is severely retarded but lateral shoots may appear and the young tree gradually recovers. If grazing causes repeated damage, the tree becomes bushy in shape without an obvious main stem and it may be many years before it develops a typical form. During this early period in the tree's life defoliation by insects is probably not very important, but when the tree is tall enough for the leaves to be out of the reach of browsing mammals the main leaf-eating role is taken over by insects, particularly the Lepidoptera.

In Great Britain caterpillars of over a hundred species of moths have been recorded as feeding on oak leaves but extensive defoliation is mostly caused by the winter moth or the green oak tortrix moth. These species also feed on oak leaves in other parts of Europe, although quite a number of other moth larvae, such as the mottled umber, the brown-tail, the buff-tip and the lackey moths, can build up to high densities and cause defoliation.

The gipsy moth is certainly a common defoliator of oak both in Europe and in the north-east of the United States, where it was introduced from Europe in the late nineteenth century. This unfortunate introduction resulted in a massive caterpillar plague which stripped the foliage from many species of forest trees and also did a great deal of damage in apple orchards. The females are quite large and may be 70 mm across, with pale, dirty-white wings, but the males are much smaller. Although the females have normal wings, they seldom use them, preferring to remain on the bark of the tree until discovered by the males. In order to attract a mate, she exudes a chemical substance that can be detected over considerable distances.

There are as many hungry insects as the foliage-eaters who attack the buds of the oak: gall wasps, gall midges, weevils and capsid bugs all exploit the unopened bud making the mortality often very high. Nevertheless the oak has a remarkable capacity to overcome these setbacks and rapidly produces more buds in spite of constant attack. It also has a strong chemical defence, in the tannins which the leaves rapidly accumulate, making them less palatable with the result that the caterpillars eat less, grow more slowly and suffer higher mortality, the adult insects, being smaller, lay fewer eggs. To some extent leaf-eating insects have adjusted to these chemical defence systems, because many more species attack the tree in the early summer when the leaves are young than in the late summer when the leaves are fully developed.

One of the insects which has exploited this suc-

Left: The oak hook-tip moth is widespread in Europe in deciduous woods where the larvae feed on the leaves of oak.

Oak galls

Almost as characteristic as the leaves and fruit of the oak are the galls, whose origin is probably not known to most casual observers. A gall is a growth which appears on part of a tree – usually a leaf, twig or bud – as a result of attack by a parasitic insect, mite or fungus, bacterium or eelworm. It is derived entirely from the tissues of the plant since it develops as a growth-reaction to the attack. The plant cells are stimulated by a chemical transferred from the insect to reproduce more rapidly than normal or else to grow to a much larger size. In this way a curious structure develops which becomes the home of the parasite. Why the tree should react in this way is not well understood, but the insect parasite may inject an irritant with her ovipositor as she pierces the tissues to lay an egg. Sometimes a gall may develop when the tissue is pierced in this way, even though an egg is not laid, but generally an egg and later a

Above: A vapourer moth sitting on its cocoon. This species is widespread in Europe and North America.

Right: Currant galls are produced on the catkins of the oak tree by a small wasp which emerges from a different sort of gall in the spring. These galls are soft and spherical and change from green to red, resembling bunches of red currants.

cessfully is the green oak-leaf roller moth, one of the most abundant insects found on oak trees throughout Europe and Asia Minor. It is quite small with attractive green fore-wings and light-brown hind-wings. The adult moths emerge usually at the end of May and become active at dusk when they fly up to the oak crowns. The fertilized female searches for a small depression on the twigs in which to deposit two eggs. She then moves on to another site until a total of fifty to sixty eggs have been laid. The eggs remain throughout the winter in their camouflaged position and in the following spring the tiny caterpillars emerge to crawl on to the nearest bud. They penetrate through the cracks in the half-open scales and feed on the new leaves as they unfold. If the caterpillars are very numerous they can almost totally defoliate a large tree. They react to disturbance by rapidly dropping down on a silk thread life-line, and make their way back when the crisis is over.

Right: Acorns are eaten by insects as well as mammals, like this larva of the small moth Cydia splendana which also will feed on walnuts.

larva seem necessary. The stimulus for the full growth of the gall seems to be a substance secreted from the digestive glands of the larva. As soon as the larva stops feeding, just before it pupates, or if it should die, the gall does not develop any further.

Most leaf and bud galls are caused by different types of insects, particularly leaf-bugs, green-flies, plant-lice, scale insects, wasps, midges, beetles and moths. Many different tree species are attacked but perhaps one of the most familiar galls is the so-called 'oak-apple', a spherical growth 2–4 cm in diameter. The oak-apple is caused by a small wasp. This has two generations and the first, which consists of asexual females, lays its eggs at the base of a leaf bud in the spring. A gall grows rapidly with the larva inside and reaches full size about mid-summer when it is pale-pink and somewhat spongy in texture. The wasps which emerge in June and July include males and females, and after mating the females penetrate

51

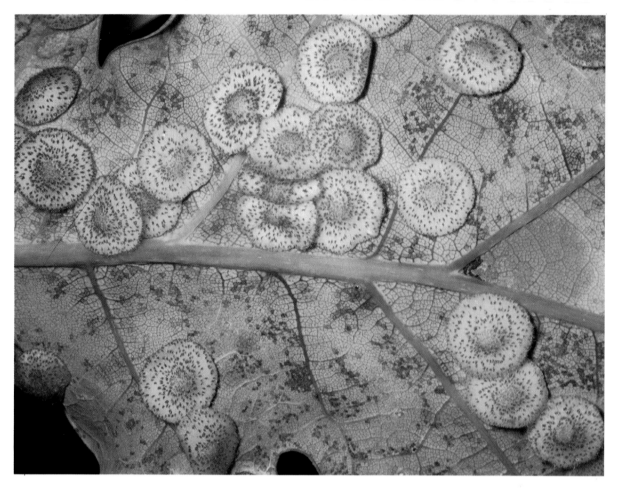

the soil adjacent to the tree and insert their eggs in the tissues of the rootlets. When the eggs hatch, root galls develop – small brownish structures about three quarters of a centimetre in diameter. As these take sixteen to seventeen months to mature, the adults, which are again all wingless females, do not emerge until after the second winter. This is the asexual part of the life-cycle because the females lay eggs which do not need to be fertilized. They crawl up the bark of the tree until they find a suitable leaf

bud for egg-laying and the whole cycle starts again.

In general, galls cause little damage to the tree and in any case the occupant is itself not always safe from parasites and predators. Small birds, particularly tits and some woodpeckers, have learned that the gall contains a juicy grub and it is relatively easy to excavate the soft tissue to reach it. Other creatures, such as certain small wasps, mites, flies, beetles and tiny moths, may also colonize the gall as lodgers and although they may not attack the original occupant, they share its food supply and may cause it to starve to death. All insects are preyed on by parasites such as chalcid wasps and ichneumonid flies, and gall-formers are no exception. These specialized insects seek out the grub, lay an egg close by and the parasitic larva then feeds directly on its host, causing its death.

The oak leaf is probably the most important source of food produced by the tree, judging from the amount consumed in the early summer and the large numbers of insects sharing this resource. A 20-metre oak might support 200,000 to 400,000 caterpillars at any one time in the summer. Apart from the larger caterpillars which may consume the whole leaf, others are tiny enough to live within the narrow leaf-blade. These are called leaf-miners and include many Lepidoptera but also some weevils, flies and Hymenoptera. The larvae of these insects often show special adaptations to this curious way of life – they may have no legs, or their minute bodies may be flattened. Each species generally makes a mine with a distinctive shape and pattern.

Leaf-miners are protected to some extent by being entirely enclosed within the two surfaces of the leaf, but larger caterpillars are exposed to the many predators which hunt throughout the tree foliage. They try to avoid detection in many different ways. Some are green to match the colour of the leaves while other remain motionless during the day and feed only under the protection of darkness. Other caterpillars make themselves inconspicuous by adopting devices to eliminate shadow. For instance, the light-emerald moth larva spends the day flattened along a twig of the same colour, blending even better because its shadow is broken up by a fringe of hairs along either side. The small caterpillars of the purple hairstreak butterfly are so coloured that they resemble the scales of the buds on the oak tree, while the caterpillar of the oak beauty moth looks just like a small twig. Adult moths and butterflies may also be remarkably well camouflaged: the comma butterfly resembles a dead oak leaf while many moths are such a perfect match for the bark or lichens of the tree trunk that they become virtually invisible. Another device used by the larvae of many leaf-feeding insects is to make a tent by rolling the leaf around them and then feed inside, away from the sharp eyes of predators.

The teeming life in the foliage of the oak attracts large numbers of carnivorous invertebrates which in turn may be eaten by birds, forming a complex food-chain. Some of the common ladybirds may be abundant where aphids are available; lacewings, mites, flower bugs and beetles all find a rich harvest of food. A particularly handsome beetle is the large *Calasoma inquisitor*, which hunts at night, seeking out leaf-feeding caterpillars. Its close relative, *C. syco-phanta*, is so active a predator that it was one of the insects imported into the U.S.A. to help control the ravaging hordes of gipsy and brown-tail moth caterpillars. A less robust but equally effective insect destroyer is the delicate oak bush-cricket. It is a graceful pale-green creature which spends most of the day motionless on the underside of a leaf. At dusk it becomes active and feeds readily on looper caterpillars, aphids and sawfly larvae and will even eat its own kind if it has the opportunity.

The most effective of the forester's insect friends is the wood-ant *Formica rufa* and its allies. In many European countries wood-ants are protected by law because they are thought to destroy so many forest insect pests and there seems to be good evidence for this. A *Formica rufa* nest may contain as many as 300,000 ants. Observations on a related species suggested that about 100,000 insects were caught each day and brought back to the nest. Wood-ants forage widely over the forest floor and will readily climb

Above left: The oak bush cricket is a delicate, graceful insect – it is entirely carnivorous, feeding on caterpillars and aphids.

53

up into the canopy of trees in their search for caterpillars, aphids or any other invertebrate they can carry back to the nest for food.

One group of predators that must not be overlooked consists of the spiders and harvestmen. Both are entirely carnivorous, and, although there are relatively few species of the latter, there are large numbers of spiders of many different types living in all forest habitats from the forest floor to the tops of trees. Small black money spiders live in the leaf litter, moss and crevices around the base of the tree; delicate webs are spun across rough furrows in the bark and throughout the foliage, twigs and branches there is a multitude of spiders of all shapes, sizes and hunting behaviour: clubionids which catch by stealth, crab-spiders which make a sudden grab and jumping spiders which stalk their prey and leap onto it like miniature lions. In high summer, when activity is at its peak, it is a remarkable experience to stand beneath the foliage of a forest tree and gently tap the branches and twigs over a beating-tray. Soon the tray will be covered by a seething mass of caterpillars, leaf-bugs, flies, beetles and spiders.

The pine processionary

The rich variety of life in deciduous trees no doubt helps to preserve an ecological balance which prevents the worst excesses of pest outbreaks, but on coniferous trees the fauna is generally poorer and insect pests can be responsible for widespread and serious damage. Throughout Europe, on many species of pine trees, the traveller will see the curious silk bags made by the processionary caterpillar, the larva of an all-too-common moth. Towards the end of July, depending on the altitude and climatic conditions, the adult moths emerge from the ground where they have pupated. After mating, the female may fly some distance to find a suitable pine tree on which to lay her eggs. These number from seventy to three hundred, and are placed in strings of about 5 cm encircling one or more pine needles and protected by a covering of fine scales scraped from the female moth's abdomen. A month later the little caterpillars appear, each with a large head and powerful jaws to grind up the tough pine needles on which they feed. They move about in the foliage of the pine, spinning little silk tents for protection while feeding. In October, having reached a good size, several caterpillars build a winter retreat where they shelter until the following spring. This is often quite large and is usually placed on the tip of a branch, from which it hangs like a white muff. French entomologist Jean Henri Fabre tells how he found the

Above: Silk nests built by the pine processionary caterpillar for protection during the winter months. The caterpillar eats the leaves of pine trees and causes considerable damage in countries bordering the Mediterranean.

Right: Oak processionary caterpillars marching in single file on a foraging expedition.

55

caterpillars to be accurate barometers and by watching their movements he knew when the wintry weather was coming. In fine winter weather they would come out of their nest each day and, following their leader, would descend the tree in procession with the nose of the second close up to the tail of the first and so on, with perhaps as many as 300 caterpillars moving down the tree. Each caterpillar made a silk thread as it walked, contributing to a broad silken highroad by which they were able to find their way back to the winter nest after their excursion. By a simple experiment Fabre demonstrated that this processionary behaviour was very strongly developed. He noticed that on one occasion the procession climbed up to the top of a large garden vase and started to walk around the rim. He quickly destroyed the silk pathway on the lower parts of the vase so that the procession continued for hour after hour and even for days, marching round the vase. Eventually they fell off exhausted. Although they appeared to be of such interest to Fabre, he certainly did not welcome their presence because they destroyed his trees, leaving them as if they had been swept by fire. Every winter he used to remove the nests with a long, forked pole.

In spring, when the caterpillars are full-grown, they leave their tree nests and return to the soil to pupate, remaining there until the late summer when the adult moths again emerge. There are at least two species of processionary caterpillar, one of which attacks oak as well as pine. Scientists have worked hard to find predators and parasites which are capable of destroying the caterpillar plagues and a virus disease has been developed which can be sprayed over forests from the air.

Another insect which is a serious forest pest in coniferous plantations is the European pine sawfly. It is widespread throughout the temperate regions of the Old World except in southern Europe and also does well in North America, where it was introduced early in the twentieth century. The body of the male insect is a glossy black with reddish tinges on the lower part of the abdomen and upper part of the thorax. The female is light orange-brown.

The life-cycle is particularly interesting. Because the species can survive the extremely cold winter of the Arctic it is able to penetrate to regions beyond the Arctic circle. The adults emerge late in the summer or early autumn when the fertilized female lays between sixty and a hundred eggs on pine needles near the top buds or annual shoots of the younger trees. The eggs are capable of withstanding the severest winter weather, even when the temperature falls to $-40°C$. The eggs hatch in the following April/May and the larvae feed on the pine needles until they pupate in mid-summer. To do this they descend to the layer of leaf litter on the forest floor, where the pupal cocoon is constructed.

Larvae of numerous other species of moths are formidable forest pests and one of the most damaging is the pine looper moth, a species widespread in Europe and Asia but which does not occur in North America. The adults appear in mid-summer and soon after mating the eggs are laid in rows on the undersides of old pine needles. The larvae hatch within two weeks and feed on the crowns of the pines, eating the needles from the top and periphery of the tree. They eat the entire needle with the exception of the midrib, and the remnant exudes resin, turns yellow and falls off. Most of the damage is done to trees twenty to seventy years old so they can severely check the growth or even kill the tree by defoliation.

Below: The landscape of southern England has been transformed by the ravages of Dutch elm disease – in many areas as much as eighty per cent of the tree population has been killed off.

Bark and wood eaters

Insect damage to the bark and wood of a tree is not usually obvious until well advanced. When a rotten branch breaks off or the bark becomes loose, revealing numerous galleries made by boring larvae, we know that infestation is widespread. The attentions of woodpeckers also indicate the presence of active larvae in or under the bark. Much of this type of damage to healthy trees is caused by different species of small beetles. One well-known group includes the ambrosia beetles, so-called because they cultivate fungi inside the galleries in order to feed on the fruiting bodies. The adult beetles bore into the bark and wood, making long cylindrical black tunnels

Right: The culprits of Dutch elm disease are grubs of the bark beetle which bore through the inner layers of bark spreading the deadly fungus which causes the disease.

Below right: The intricate patterns of the bark beetles' galleries.

about the diameter of a pencil lead. The eggs are laid in clusters and it is possible to find larvae, pupae and adults all together in the same series of galleries. The fungus they introduce grows on the faecal pellets of the adults and larvae and is responsible for the black colour of the tunnel walls.

Another important family of beetles are the Scolytidae, or bark beetles, of which there are many species. They are generally rather small, ranging from 1–7 mm, and excavate easily recognised tunnel systems between the bark and the wood of the tree. The tunnel patterns are so intricate and characteristic that the insects are familiarly called 'engraver beetles'. The female cuts a short entrance hole in the bark of a tree which leads into the main tunnel, known as the pairing chamber, where

57

mating of the polygamous species takes place. From it a number of mother tunnels radiate out in different directions, the whole system being shaped like a star. The female deposits her eggs along the sides of these galleries in small niches specially cut for this purpose.

The physical damage caused by bark beetles is not in itself generally very serious and there seems to be some evidence that they usually attack a tree which is already in a sickly condition. But the elm bark beetles, of which there are two well-known species, have been responsible for an enormous mortality of trees because they transmit the fungus that causes the notorious Dutch elm disease. In this case the association between the beetle and the fungus seems to be fortuitous. The beetle simply acts as a carrier for the fungus, enabling it to grow in the most favourable area of the tree. The fungus spreads rapidly throughout the trunk and branches and prevents the flow of sap to the leaves and small twigs, which soon die and begin to fall. It is thought that the recent epidemic in Britain stems largely from an importation of a virulent strain from North America, where it is reported that four and a quarter million elm trees died from 1933 to 1940. The original home of the disease is not known but since 1927 it has spread across Britain, although it did not cause extensive damage until the 1970s. By 1978, in central and southern England, over fifteen million elms had died of the disease.

Wood wasps and their enemies

Other insects which utilize living timber are the large and strikingly coloured wood wasps, whose larvae damage trees such as Scots pine, larch and spruce. The yellow-and-black wood wasp is a handsome insect, often mistaken for a hornet, which it resembles when flying. Fortunately it does not have a sting. A second species is steel-blue in colour and is common on larch and silver fir. The adults of these insects are in flight from June until the autumn and are particularly active in bright sunlight, when their large transparent wings make a noisy whirring sound. The females have an ovipositor as long as 2 cm. This consists of three parts, two of them slender vertical saws with which the insect bores a tunnel into solid wood. The construction of the tunnel takes about eight to ten minutes and inside it the insect lays from five to seven eggs. After about four weeks the young larvae hatch and begin to cut their first tunnel at right angles to the egg tunnel, into the superficial layers of the wood. As they excavate they fill up the tunnel behind them with discarded wood particles, which are tightly rammed together by the sharp spine at the rear of the body. When the larva is about half-grown it penetrates deep into the wood and in the smaller trees it may actually reach into the heart of the timber. The larva grows slowly and is not ready to pupate for some two-and-a-half to three years. Five to six weeks after pupation the

adult insect cuts its way out of the wood, emerging through a circular hole. Although these insects can cause formidable damage they, like the bark beetles, do not as a rule attack healthy trees. They usually choose those which for one reason or another have been weakened, perhaps by an attack of fungus or physical damage.

The wood wasp has a number of interesting parasites which undoubtedly help to regulate its population. The most impressive of these is an ichneumonid fly of remarkable size, varying in length from 2.5 to 10 cm, measured from the tip of the antennae to the end of the very long ovipositor. The interesting thing about this parasite is that it attacks the larva of the wood wasp, in spite of it being deep within the wood of the tree. It is not an easy prey to reach. The

Left: The elegant ichneumon fly Rhyssa persuasoria *lays her eggs on the larva of the wood wasp. What is amazing apart from the hole-drilling operation carried out by means of her specially adapted and long ovipositor, is the precision with which she can detect her prey, apparently safe within the tree trunk. It is thought that the ichneumon fly detects the wood wasp's movements by ultra-sensitive detectors on her antennae.*

parasite first has to find the exact location of the larva and then penetrate the wood in order to lay an egg on it. The female ichneumonid searches the logs using its sensitive antennae, which somehow tell it precisely where the unsuspecting larva is situated. Having selected the exact spot, the insect raises its wings, arches its abdomen and the long ovipositor is then raised with the help of one of the hind-legs. With the abdomen held high, the ovipositor moves up and down with incredible rapidity and the thin vertical saws in the basal portion soon cut a hole in the solid wood to a depth of 3 cm or more. The whole process takes about twenty minutes – an excellent opportunity to observe the remarkable behaviour of this insect.

Once the hole has been completed the fly inserts the ovipositor to its full length and the eggs can then pass down onto the body of the wood wasp larva, possibly after it has been stung to cause partial paralysis. This would quieten the larva so that the frail ichneumon egg can be placed in exactly the right position. The eggs hatch in about two days and a larva about 2 mm long emerges. After roaming about on the body of the host it settles down and begins to suck the juices of its victim with its prominent jaws. In a little over three weeks the parasite has reduced the wood wasp larva to an empty shell. It remains in its host's tunnel for the rest of the summer and throughout autumn and winter, pupating in the spring of the following year. After a few weeks the adult insect emerges and cuts her way out of the timber.

Left: Pairing between the smaller male and larger female cicada, Cicadetta montana. Cicadas are sap-sucking insects, confined mainly to warm regions though the species shown is found in a restricted area of southern England.

cicadas

...he bizarre and astonishing seem to be normal ...aracteristics of insect life-cycles, and none more so ...an the cicada's, whose larvae are born in the timber ... the standing tree but pass most of their develop-...ental period in the soil. In Europe cicadas are in-...cts of the south, particularly the Mediterranean ...rests from Spain, France and east into Asia.

...Although the continuous reeling song of these ...sects is so characteristic of forests in late summer, ...ere are relatively few species in Europe compared ...th tropical regions. The majority live on trees of ...e sort of another although the species which ex-...nds furthest north in Europe is believed to feed ...gely on bracken.

...The cicada song, which is characteristic for each ...ecies, is produced by small membranes called tym-...ls, situated in two resonating cavities, one on each ...e of the abdomen and vibrated rapidly by the ...cion of tiny muscles. It is a method of sound pro-...ction almost unique among insects. Although ...nilar organs are found among leaf-hoppers, which ... related to cicadas, they do not produce anything ...e the same volume of sound. In the hot days of ...e summer the song appears to come from every ...rection in the tree canopy.

...Although the cicadas are large insects, their adult ...e does not exceed four or five weeks. During this time the female bores a hole into dry timber where she deposits some forty eggs. After about three months the very small larva emerges and makes its way outwards, so that with the approach of winter it is near the surface of the bark. The larvae pass their first moult in the burrow and then the second instar larvae descend to the soil on a silk thread. Careful examination of a larva will show that it has a strongly developed first pair of legs which it uses to burrow into the ground, where it feeds on the small rootlets of the host tree. It remains in the soil for four years, though an American species is known to stay as long as seventeen. During this time it roams about in the soil, responding to the soil temperature and looking for food. When the larva has completed its seventh instar it prepares to emerge by constructing a little corridor to the surface of the soil which it lines with a hard cement-like material. Then one warm night when hopefully the many predators are not actively searching in the neighbourhood, the nymph crawls out of the ground and climbs as high as it can on a tree trunk, where it attaches itself beneath a branch. The next day the skin splits and the new cicada, a beautiful green, appears. When the sun rises and the heat of the day spreads through the forest, she takes to flight for her brief life. Adult cicadas do not eat but pierce the bark of a twig or branch and drink the sap which oozes out.

Far left: The female cicada lays her groups of eggs in slits made in the bark with her ovipositor.

Left: The first instar of the young cicada larva emerging from the egg nest.

Left: After several years living on rootlets in the soil, the fifth instar of the cicada emerges from the ground and pupates on a tree trunk.

The agents of decay

When we walk through a modern planted woodland, we notice in particular its tidiness and uniformity and so it would be easy to assume that a forest with dead trees and fallen timber was neglected and impoverished. The dead wood that accumulates on the forest floor under natural conditions, however, may amount to a considerable proportion of the total timber and is an important food resource for animal life. In Great Britain over a thousand species of animals are known to occur in dead and dying wood and 456 of these can be found in one 400 hectare woodland alone near Oxford.

If a tree or branch in a temperate forest falls in an open, exposed place, where the sun and the wind can dry it out, it becomes almost fossilized with very little decay taking place and the colonization by the insect fauna is very slow. Such logs persist for many years. If, on the other hand, as is normally the case, a log falls in a damp shady place under the canopy of the tree, then the colonization by fungi and insects is much quicker and the whole process of decomposition may go through its various stages at a rapid rate. Some of the first to arrive are scolytid beetles, which make their galleries under the bark, and also longhorn beetles which burrow straight into the timber. At the same time the moist log is attacked directly by fungal decay under the bark, greatly helped by the activities of the different boring insects. It is interesting to note, however, that beech seems to have no beetles adapted to exploiting its bark and it may take two years or more before it reaches the stage of cracking and loosening so fungi and insects can penetrate underneath. By this time numerous invertebrate animals will have colonized, including woodlice, millipedes, centipedes, spiders, pseudoscorpions, earwigs, collembola, the larvae of flies and beetles. Some of these eat wood while others feed on the microflora of fungi and algae. As the process of decay proceeds, the initial colonists disappear and different species take their place. These later species tend to be generalists, in the sense that they are able to live on the wood of many different trees. When a large tree becomes weakened internally by heart-rot usually brought about by fungus, it is not uncommon for its crown to break right off, leaving a standing trunk. The wood in the centre of the tree soon rots away, leaving a hollow trunk, although the outer sapwood is still alive. In this way another habitat is created for woodland life, both invertebrate and vertebrate.

Death in a tree is quite a different matter from death in an animal. A tree which is partly dead or in an advanced stage of decay can survive for a very long period. For example, the bristle-cone pine in California, the oldest living thing in the world, often appears to be almost entirely dead. One of the secrets of its longevity is its ability to retard its growth by allowing all but a small portion of the tree to die.

Many of these old pines seem to be devoid of ba and yet there will be a small strand of living tiss which, like a lifeline twisting round the tree, enab it to continue living and produce leaves.

In the tropics the breakdown processes are rapid that fallen wood and litter seldom accumula and there are also many insects which help to acc erate this process. In the warm climate of the southe

Right: Where there is death there is life, exemplified by this giant beech tree which as it rots provides support and nourishment for a variety of plant life.

62

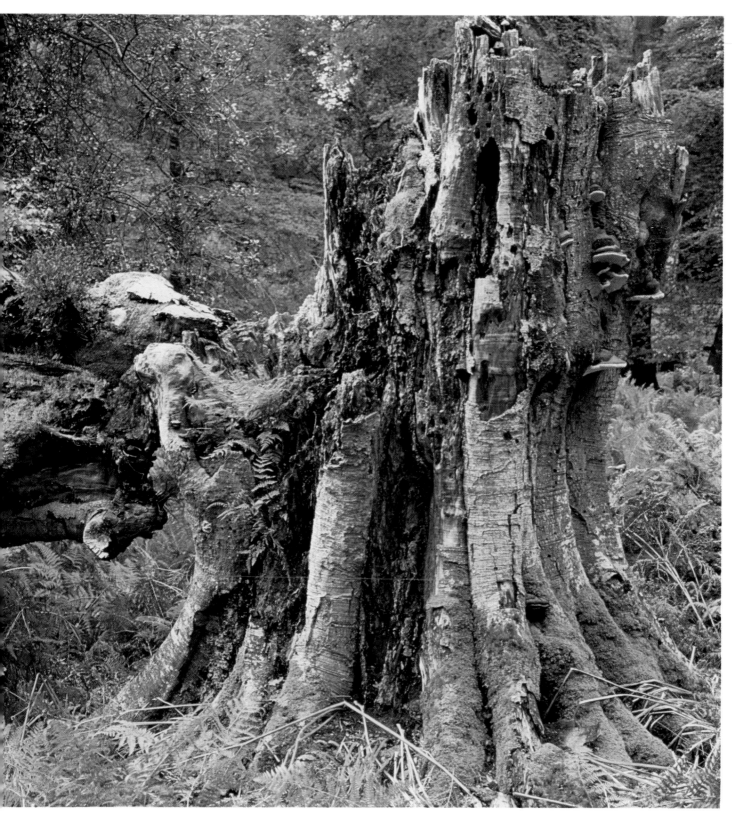

emperate region, for example in North Carolina in the United States, the dead material is broken down in a period of three years. As we go north, the process gradually becomes slower. In the great forest of Kubany Wald in central Europe, where the winters are cold and the summers hot, the volume of standing and fallen timber is about equal to that which is living. In the Swiss National Park, which consists chiefly of coniferous trees, about a quarter of the twenty million trees and about a third of the estimated volume of standing timber, is dying or dead. In fact many northern coniferous forests have a dense layer of fallen timber because the low temperatures inhibit decomposition. Amber, a fossil tree resin, is the product of coniferous forest decomposition; large deposits occur along the shores of the Baltic.

FOREST BIRDS

Compared with the raucous and exotic birds calls of tropical forests, temperate forests are an almost silent experience. This is especially true in winter, or in late summer when one is more aware of the buzz of insects than actual bird song. In fact, the familiar bird life of temperate forests is adjusted to the clear-cut seasonality of food supply and the few species which remain during the cold months of the year are able to exploit the resources which would not be available to the summer visitors. Resident birds such as titmice, tree creepers and the wren are very small and spend much time searching the trunks and branches of the leafless trees, taking eggs and grubs of overwintering insects as well as small spiders and collembola from crevices in the bark. Woodpeckers excavate for beetle grubs hiding in their galleries under the bark and in rotting wood, while siskins and redpolls eat seeds, berries and buds as well as any insects they come across. Larger resident birds such as jays and nutcrackers feed on nuts, berries, acorns and a great variety of small animal life. The nutcracker and the crossbill, which feeds mostly on pine seeds, sometimes travel considerable distances in those years when there is a shortage of seeds in their home ranges. Another species well-known for this behaviour is the waxwing, a beautiful pinky-brown bird with a prominent crest, which lives in the northern coniferous forests in both the Old and New Worlds. In the winter it feeds mainly on berries and if the local supply is poor, large numbers migrate to regions where food is more plantiful. A second and smaller species, the cedar waxwing, occurs widely in North America, but this is a bird of mainly deciduous woods, large gardens and orchards, where it sometimes takes too many of the early cherries.

As the days grow longer and warmer, the migrants sweep north again. The forest colours are brightened by the pale green of the first leaves emerging from the opening buds. It is one of the most attractive times of the year. The sun's rays still penetrate through the open canopy and light the spring flowers on the forest floor, where they are visited by butterflies emerging after winter hibernation. Soon the forest rings with birdsong; breeding territories are established, nests are built and eggs laid – all carefully timed so that the young can be fed when insects are most abundant. This is especially so in the deciduous forest, where the change from a winter to a summer aspect is most marked. It is not so striking in the coniferous woodland because most of the trees retain their leaves all through the year. There are a few exceptions, however, such as the larch, which produces a fresh crop of leaves each spring, while all the evergreen conifers take on spring colours when the tufts of new leaves appear among the darker green of last year's foliage.

Left: The bristle cone pine, a native of western North America is the oldest living tree, and also has an extremely low rate of growth.

Right: The chiffchaff is an attractive warbler named after its rather monotonous call of 'chiff-chaff' or 'zip-zap'. It breeds in northern Europe and overwinters in Africa.

The North American coniferous forest is richer in birdlife than similar forest in Europe, probably because there are many more species of trees with a better understorey and thus a greater range of habitat diversity. In particular there are many more summer migrants, principally warblers, which nest in the evergreen forest. One of the most striking is the American redstart which, in spite of its name, is not related to the European redstarts. It has a similar white, black and red plumage and it is not surprising that the early European settlers thought it was a relation of the familiar bird they knew back home. The sight of its brilliant plumage against the dark-green foliage of the forest delights all birdwatchers seeing it for the first time. Its feeding behaviour recalls that of the flycatcher because it takes most of its insect prey in the air, darting out from its perch in the canopy. Other warblers of the spruce, fir and pine forests of America include the pine-creeping warbler, which prefers the pitch pine, the black-throated green warbler, which is partial to white pine, and the magnolia warbler, which likes red or white spruce. There are many more species, too numerous to mention.

Feeding behaviour

In contrast, the warblers found in European coniferous woodlands are generally small greenish or brownish birds, without the striking colours of those in North America. These birds are generally known as leaf-warblers because most of their food-hunting is confined to the foliage, whereas other birds feed on bark or timber insects, or else in the leaf litter on the ground. This is all part of a well-marked zonation of feeding niches among woodland birds. There is some overlap but in general serious competition is avoided and so the forest is able to support more birds than would otherwise be possible.

In the mixed broadleaved and coniferous forests in Britain the goldcrest generally occupies the highest parts of the canopy, the coal and blue tits the middle zone, the willow and long-tailed tits lower still, while the larger great tits spend much time feeding on the ground. Nevertheless when there is an abundance of food, many different species may feed together, as for instance during a plague of pine moth caterpillars. Seasonal differences also occur. In a broadleaved woodland during the summer the European blue tit hunts for food mainly on the leaves, but in the autumn and early winter it switches to dead branches and twigs. Later in the winter and in the spring it spends most of its time searching for insects on the buds. Similarly the greater spotted woodpecker in Finland was found to feed almost exclusively on pine-cone seeds in winter while in the summer ants and other insects formed the bulk of its diet. In this study a woodpecker was watched during the whole of one October day, when it collected 137 pine cones. Each cone was wedged in a crevice, usu-

ally between two branches of a tree, and the seeds were extracted. It was estimated that the bird ate 170 seeds per hour over an 11-hour day. This is a high rate of feeding and usually more characteristic of smaller birds which must search for food continuously during the short winter days. Leaf warblers and other birds of this size will die of starvation if deprived of food for twenty-four hours, while their nestlings would not survive at most more than a few hours.

Many birds tide over periods of shortage by collecting food when it is abundant and storing it. One of the best examples of this is the thick-billed nutcracker which, in Sweden, feeds its young primarily on hazel nuts. The bird gathers nuts in the autumn and stores them until the spring so that it is able to

Above: The long-tailed tit, a common woodland bird, makes a distinctive domed egg-shaped nest made from mosses, lichens and cobwebs

66

feed its nestlings even when snow is still on the ground and nuts have disappeared from the bushes. The hiding places are memorized and each nutcracker is able to find only its own nut stores and not those of other birds. Where the stone pine is common, as in the Swiss National Park, the nutcracker tears off the cones and digs into the scales to extract the large seed or nut. These it swallows until the crop is swollen with thirty or more. It then flies off until it finds a small clearing where there is a little grass among the bilberry bushes. Here it rapidly bores a hole and drops in six to twelve nuts, carefully covering them with earth or stones and finally a few pine needles. It then moves on a little way and does the same again until its crop is entirely empty. In this way the nutcracker is able to prepare hundreds of little hiding places during the autumn as food stores for the time when no pine cones are left on the trees. It has been observed that as many as three to four hundred nut larders might be prepared by an individual bird. It is able to remember the location of nearly all these, although it may be months before it needs to retrace it steps and go back for the food.

Food can be a limiting factor between species which share the same resource. Some interesting examples are known of ecological separation of related species having similar food requirements. In western Europe the coal tit is characteristic of coniferous trees and the blue tit of broadleaved woodlands, but in the Canary Islands the coal tit is absent while the blue tit is common not only in broadleaved trees but also in pinewoods. A parallel case occurs in the chaffinch, of which there is only one species in Europe. It is widespread in coniferous and deciduous forests. On the islands of Gran Canaria and Teneriffe, however, there are two species, the common and the blue chaffinch. The former is found only in broadleaved woods while the latter is confined to the pinewoods. On the nearby island of Palma, the blue chaffinch is missing and in this case the common chaffinch has extended through all types of woodland, both broadleaved and coniferous.

Below: The European nutcracker is a true forest bird, it feeds on the seeds of coniferous trees and also hazelnuts. It is found in the Alps, Scandinavia east to Siberia.

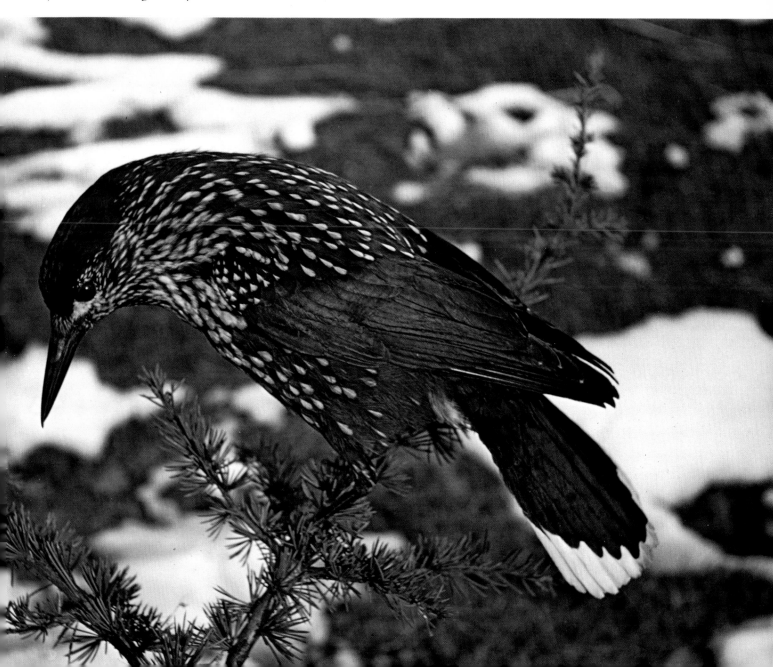

Woodpeckers and sapsuckers

Adaptation to forest life by birds is influenced by many factors, although food supply is regarded as the most important. We have seen that some species are able to change to different types of food material as one source declines and another increases, while other birds such as crossbills, waxwings and nutcrackers may disperse widely to new areas or store food during times of abundance. Woodpeckers and their allies display several of these characteristics, although much still needs to be discovered about their behaviour and biology. Only nine species breed regularly in European temperate forests and the two largest are the green and the black woodpeckers. The black woodpecker is the larger of the two and about the size of a crow. It is entirely black except for a red cap to the head in the male and a small patch of red on the nape of the female. It has a loud, fluty call, rather mournful in tone, which carries over a great distance in the forested valleys of the mountains. It is mainly a bird of conifers but will also breed in deciduous woodland, particularly beech. Its food consists largely of nuts, supplemented in winter by the larvae of beetles which it excavates from the wood and bark of trees.

The green woodpecker also feeds largely on ants, but they are taken mainly on the ground, particularly in open grassy areas. This species is not really a forest bird but prefers the woodland edge, scattered trees in a parkland situation and small copses where there are individual large trees providing suitable nest sites. In some parts of Europe, as more land goes under the plough, the disappearance of grassland where ants are numerous has probably been as much responsible for the decline in numbers of green woodpeckers as the destruction of trees. Both black and green woodpeckers must excavate large holes for nest construction and although this is sometimes done in sound timber, most nest holes are made in trees where some of the wood is already decayed.

In North America the large pileated woodpecker also feeds on ants, but in this case it excavates extensive holes in trees in its search for the black wood-boring ant which often attacks live trees, starting from the roots and tunnelling into the heartwood far up into the stem. This woodpecker not only requires well-grown trees for its nest site but the timber must also be of the type favoured by the ant. Perhaps this type of specialization is the reason why this woodpecker is rare, while smaller and more generalized feeders such as the downy and hairy woodpeckers are more widespread.

The greater spotted woodpecker is a medium-sized bird, about the same as a song thrush. It is much more a true forest bird than the green woodpecker and occurs in both deciduous and coniferous woodland. In the temperate parts of western Europe it is mainly an insect feeder, taking beetles and their grubs in bark and timber, but as we have seen in Scandinavia, its winter diet consists largely of the seeds of spruce and pine. Its adaptability may be one reason why it is a widespread and common species throughout most of Europe. Apart from insects and seeds it also likes to drink the sap of trees rather like the American group of woodpeckers called the sapsuckers. It excavates a ring of holes along a horizontal line around the trunk of the tree, forming part of, or a complete, circle. The sap oozes from the bark and the woodpecker visits it from time to time to drink. Even the resinous sap of pine trees is palatable. Many insects are also attracted to the sap springs and provide the birds with an additional source of food. The wounds caused by this method of feeding heal in the course of time but the individual scars can be seen for many years. The same sort of behaviour has been recorded in the much scarcer three-toed woodpecker of Europe.

The sapsuckers of North America include several

Below: The black woodpecker is the largest of Old World woodpeckers reaching 46 cm in length. Although widespread throughout central and northern Europe, it is not easy to find because of its shy and retiring nature.

Right: A yellow-bellied sapsucker at its nest hole – a bird of the eastern forests of North America.

species, of which the yellow-bellied and red-breasted are widespread and well known. The cut-throated sapsucker is much more local, being mainly confined to mountain forests and reaching only British Columbia in Canada. The sapsucker tongue is short and modified at the tip into a sort of brush instead of the sharp, barbed spear typical of those woodpeckers feeding on insects, which have to probe into the larval galleries in order to extract the grubs. The sapsucker prefers trunks and branches which have a smooth bark and which they girdle with rows of small squarish pits regularly spaced in horizontal lines and penetrating both outer and inner barks to the sapwood underneath. Several trees may be attacked in this way so, by visiting them in turn as the sap exudes, they can obtain a regular supply of food. Insect visitors to the sap springs are also eaten. The damage caused may sometimes be considerable, mainly by weakening the tree and by making it possible for fungal diseases to penetrate, but unless repeatedly and severely attacked, the trees soon re-cover. The wounds produce woody growths, staining the timber, with the result that its market value is reduced.

Above: Sapsuckers bore small holes in the bark of trees and feed on the living sap and on the insects attracted to it. These holes were made by the yellow-bellied sapsucker, one of the most common North American species.

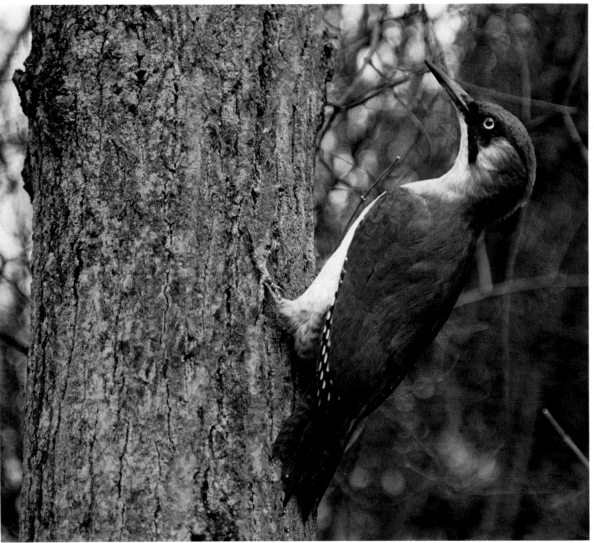

Left: Although the green woodpecker is shown here in typical woodpecker stance, it also feeds on the ground where it is particularly fond of eating ants.

which is so high-pitched that some human ears cannot detect it. They often hang upside down on a twig while searching the underside and hover rather like a humming bird as they select some food morsel from a leaf surface. The ruby-crowned kinglet is the same size but is immediately distinguished by its loud and characteristic song, which has been described as one of Nature's surprises. It is so loud and clear that one wonders how so tiny a bird can produce such a volume of sound.

Although the European goldcrest and the North American golden-crowned kinglet are separate species, it has been suggested that the original form evolved in the Old World and reached America across the land bridge which connected Alaska and Asia up to the Pleistocene age. Two subspecies have evolved in North America but both show a clear preference for evergreen forest, as does the Old World form. There are other species of birds in the coniferous forest of North America which may have originated in the same way, because they have closely related counterparts in Europe and Asia. These include the three-toed woodpeckers, the pine grosbeaks, Canada jays, brown creepers, red-breasted nuthatches and chickadees.

The last of these, the chickadees, are the North American counterparts of the familiar European titmice. The name is derived from the call of one of the most characteristic of these birds, the widespread black-capped chickadee. They are welcomed by the orchard farmer and forester alike because of the large number of harmful insects they eat. The chickadee's food is said to be 68 per cent insects and 32 per cent vegetable, the latter consisting of small seeds and various wild fruits and berries. They soon become tame in the presence of Man, just as the blue tit and great tit do in Europe, and can easily be enticed to the garden bird table, particularly during the winter months when they eagerly make the most of a lump of suet or other titbit which may be offered. The black-cap chickadee is similar in appearance to the coal tit of Europe and the latter and the crested tit are two of the most characteristic birds in coniferous woodland. The crested tit is extremely scarce in Britain, however, and practically confined to the ancient Caledonian pine forests in central Scotland. In spite of the fact that extensive new forests have been planted throughout Scotland, this bird has not yet made a serious attempt to colonize them, although elsewhere in Europe it is widespread in man-made forests as well as more ancient woodlands.

Parties of titmice are often accompanied by the tree creeper and, similarly, in America its counterpart the brown creeper may keep company with flocks of chickadees. Both the Old and New World creepers are small birds, not quite as large as a great tit, specially adapted to feeding on the bark of trees. They creep up the trunk, starting near the base, ascending with a jerky movement and looking

Agile insect eaters

Although sapsucker birds are not represented in Europe, other groups of woodland birds have ecological counterparts on each continent. The goldcrest and firecrest of Europe are wren-sized birds, the goldcrest confined mainly to coniferous forests while the firecrest is more widely distributed in broadleaved and coniferous forests. Each builds a pretty domed nest suspended beneath the foliage at the end of a branch. The goldcrest uses moss and spiders' webs for its main structure and then lines the inside with feathers. The nest is therefore very soft and well insulated. Both species are insectivorous with narrow, pointed bills. They search the foliage and twigs in the tree canopy for eggs, larvae, aphids and other small invertebrates. In the American forests two very similar birds occur – the golden-crowned kinglet, which is closely related to the European goldcrest, and the ruby-crowned kinglet, belonging to an entirely different genus. The golden-crowned kinglet behaves just like a goldcrest, moving in parties through the upper parts of the canopy and calling a continuous, fine, sharp note, *tse, tse, tse,* rather like a small mouse. They probe in the bark crevices, seeking small insects and spiders, but their delicate sickle-shaped beak is quite unsuitable for digging out timber-boring larvae as woodpeckers do. Nevertheless, the brown creeper is known to excavate small depressions in the soft bark of the giant sequoia in North America, just large enough for it to roost in. Some of the largest sequoias have numerous roosting hollows of this type. Strangely enough, the European tree creeper has also developed this roosting behaviour in the sequoia, which was not introduced to Europe until the mid-nineteenth century. But the giant sequoia is a fast-growing tree and as soon as it reached the right size the tree creepers were quick to discover how to exploit this new habitat.

Birds of prey

The large number of small and medium-sized birds which exploit the resources of the forest are them-selves eaten by larger predators. There are two groups – the owls, which are largely nocturnal and feed mainly on the small mammals in the forest, and the hawks and falcons, which are mostly bird-feeders. Other birds of prey such as buzzards and kites utilize trees for nesting purposes but range much more widely in search of food. This may consist of birds, mammals, carrion or even insects, as in the case of the honey buzzard, which seeks out the nests of wasps and bees.

Two of the most characteristic woodland hawks in Europe, the sparrowhawk and the goshawk, are now both relatively scarce over much of their range, partly because the hunter believes they compete with him for game birds and so shoots them, but also as a result of the modern use of toxic chemicals which have been passed on to the birds of prey through the smaller seed-eaters forming their principal food source. The sparrowhawk in particular has suffered in this way. Prior to 1940, for example, it was still

Right: A goshawk's nest with three nestlings approximately four weeks old.

Left: The American kestrel nests in hollow trees or the abandoned nest holes of woodpeckers. It feeds mainly on insects but will take small birds and rodents.

72

Left: The sparrowhawk, a smaller relative of the goshawk was formerly very common in Europe Persecution by gamekeepers and the widespread use of toxic agricultural chemicals in the 1950s and 1960s has contributed to its decline.

Right: The osprey is a distinctive bird of prey with an almost world-wide distribution — nesting on all the major land masses of the world except South America. It feeds almost exclusively on fish, and makes a large rough-looking nest of twigs and branches.

reasonably common in Britain and able to hold its own against the gamekeeper, but during the following decade, when there was a great expansion of the use of persistent insecticides, its numbers began to drop considerably. Apart from some regions in Europe, where toxic chemicals have never been widely used, its numbers are still at a very low ebb. Fortunately there are a few signs of recovery now that less persistent chemicals are used.

The sparrowhawk shows a preference for coniferous woodlands or plantations for nest building, and this is probably one reason why it is more numerous at the present time in areas where these woods predominate. It likes plenty of cover and so will also nest in thickets and scrub where there are few large trees. The nest is often built on an abandoned nest of a crow, magpie, jay or woodpigeon, new material being added to the old foundation. The sparrowhawk is almost entirely a predator on small birds, taking anything from a goldcrest to a starling, thrush or blackbird. When hunting it flies fast and low along wood borders, hedgerows, fences or forest rides. Typically it glides with three to four wing beats at long intervals. When hunting along a hedgerow it slips over from one side to the other every twenty to thirty metres, ready to pounce on any unsuspecting small bird. On other occasions it will fly with remarkable dexterity through the secondary growth of a wood or copse. Sometimes it keeps watch at places where birds congregate, suddenly diving down to take its prey before the bird realizes what is happening. Although it is so adept at catching

by surprise, if this manoeuvre does not immediately succeed it will chase its prey with great determination and has been known to enter houses or accidentally strike the side of a moving vehicle while in hot pursuit.

The goshawk, which looks very much like a huge sparrowhawk, preys on birds the size of a woodpigeon, jay, crow or magpie and occurs in the same type of country as the sparrowhawk, breeding in both coniferous and deciduous woods. It uses the same nest from year to year, each time with additions, and this soon becomes very bulky. In Europe it seems to prefer regions where the woodland is bordered by, or interspersed with, fields or other open ground. It will also nest in quite small woods, provided gamekeepers do not interfere with it. Unfortunately it is regarded as an enemy of woodland game and has been widely destroyed, even in countries where it is protected by law. In its hunting flights it combines speed and a perfect control of movement, the broad wings and long tail enabling it to thread its way swiftly among tree trunks or other obstacles and to check its course or to perform abrupt turns with the greatest of ease. Both the goshawk and the sparrowhawk have broad, rounded wings, a characteristic of woodland hawks which gives them perfect control. Other raptors which hunt in the open and catch their prey by swift flight generally have narrow, pointed wings.

Both the goshawk and the sparrowhawk have their closely related counterparts in North America. The American goshawk breeds in hardwood forests, irch, poplar, maple and oak and also in pine, spruce nd fir, building a bulky nest often at a considerable eight. Its food includes the woodchuck, hare, cottontail rabbit, lemming, muskrat, squirrels, together with a large variety of birds. Occasionally it will also at insects such as locusts and grasshoppers.

Most birds of prey nest in trees, apart from, for xample, the golden eagle whose haunts are in the mountains and whose nest site is usually on an inaccessible rock ledge. The American bald eagle and the osprey or fishhawk are tree-nesting birds, but hunt over water, not in the forest. The white head and tail of the bald eagle are so distinctive that it cannot be mistaken for any other large bird of prey. Perhaps this is the reason why it was adopted by the United States Congress in 1782 as the national emblem. In pite of this honour the law gave it no protection and or many years it had to face every hunter's gun because of its alleged destruction of salmon. By 1940 t had declined in numbers to such an extent that Congress passed an Act of protection applicable hroughout the country, except for Alaska, in order o save it from extinction. Protection in Alaska did iot come until 1952.

The osprey is a good deal smaller than the bald agle and lives entirely on freshwater fish. It nests in pine trees and is a distinctive bird of both European and North American coniferous forests where there are scattered lakes. The plumage is mainly brown and white but the feet are pale-blue and the soles are covered with sharp horny processes, enabling it to take a firm grip on slippery fish which it catches by diving into the surface of the water. The head is largely white with black ear coverts and there is an attractive loose crest on white dark-tipped feathers on the nape. It returns each year to the same nest site, adding more and more material until eventually the nest can grow to an enormous size. In Britain the hunter was responsible for wiping out this bird as a breeding species late in the nineteenth century and it was not until 1955 that a breeding pair appeared in Scotland. The first attempts were unsuccessful but in 1959 three young were reared. Since then public interest and concern for its survival as well as patient work by conservation organizations has enabled it to spread to other parts of Scotland.

In flight the osprey is an impressive and graceful bird, rising with motionless wings over the water, sometimes to a considerable height, pausing perhaps for a moment before dropping suddenly to the water surface. It falls, not straight down like a kingfisher, but in a long spiral so that it strikes the surface

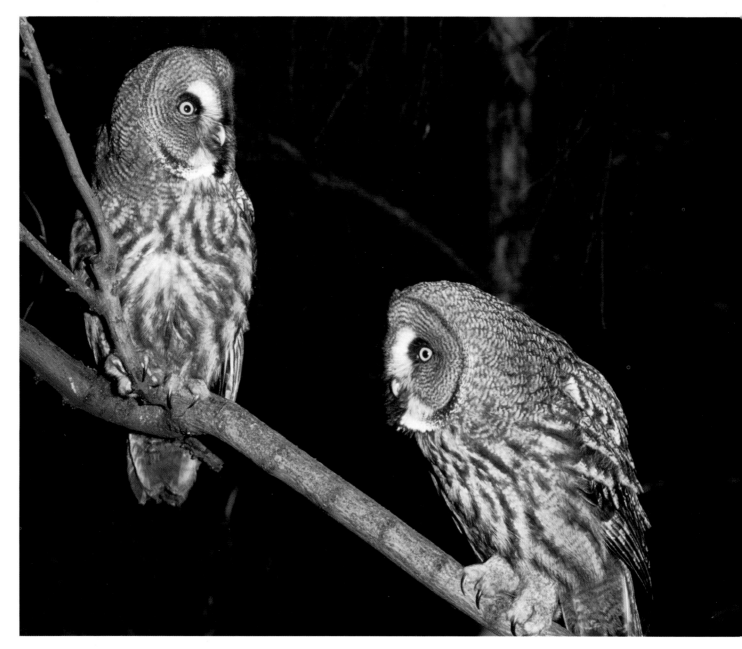

of the water with the feet first and the wings raised high above the head. There is a sudden splash of white spray and for a moment the bird, except for its black wing-tips, seem to be entirely hidden from view. Then with a heave of its powerful shoulders it raises itself clear of the water and in one or two wing beats rises into the air with the fish clasped in its rough talons.

Both the bald eagle and the osprey have been adversely affected by toxic chemicals which have accumulated in freshwater lakes. In the case of ospreys in Scandinavia this was due to the use of mercury compounds in wood-pulp factories supplying material for the paper industry. These chemicals are used to prevent the growth of fungus on the pulp but the effluents from the process run into the lakes and contaminate the fish on which the ospreys feed, with the result that their breeding success falls and the population declines considerably.

Nocturnal hunters

Owls range in size from the splendid eagle owl, which is found in both Old and New Worlds and may reach a length of 71 cm, to the little pigmy owl, of which the European species, with a length of only 16.5 cm, is slightly smaller than its North American counterpart. The great grey owl is almost as large as the eagle owl and is also found in both continents. Both species range widely throughout the northern coniferous forests. The medium-sized owls include the barn owl, not strictly a forest bird, the long-eared owl and the widespread tawny owl. All owls have soft feathers with long filaments on the barbules which dampen down the noise of the wing beat. They can therefore fly silently as they hunt, giving them the advantage of surprise as they pounce on an unsuspecting prey.

The eagle owl has been much persecuted because of its large size and attempts are being made in a

Above: The great grey owl is the most striking looking of several species of owls inhabiting the great taiga forest. It often hunts during the day, feeding on moderately sized mammals such as lemmings and squirrels.

Right: The eagle owl, named 'le grand duc' in French, is the largest and most powerful European owl. It hunts at dawn and dusk and will take prey as large as roe deer.

number of countries to protect the small relict populations and to reintroduce birds from captive stock into areas from where it has disappeared. This owl survives in the ravines and wooded valleys of the Cevennes in France, particularly in the National Park, where it haunts the rural rubbish dumps which are good hunting grounds for the brown rat. This is a favourite prey of these magnificent brids, although they will also take much larger animals. The recorded prey includes hare, rabbit, hamster, squirrel, mice and voles, hedgehog, weasel, cat and birds as large as the capercaillie, partridge, crows, moorhens and other water birds. It is even said to be able to kill small roe deer. Perhaps because of its large size, it does not always nest in tree holes but perfers to make a scrape in a hollow on the ground or on a rock ledge in a sheltered gully. It hunts mainly at dusk but like many other owls is quite prepared to go out during the day. In the summer in northern Europe beyond the Arctic circle, it must spend most of its hunting time in daylight because of the midnight sun. The diet of owls and other birds of prey is a relatively easy study because after their meals they eject the indigestible material in the form of a pellet, which is generally dropped from a regularly used perching post. The accumulated pellets can be recovered for analysis.

In a mixed deciduous wood the tawny owl was shown to feed mainly on woodmice and bank voles, which together made up about sixty per cent of the vertebrates eaten. These two were taken in equal proportions but the diet also included short-tailed voles, common shrews, moles, some small birds, insects and earthworms. It has very acute hearing and usually catches its prey by dropping on to it from its perch where it is watching and listening.

A detailed study over a period of thirteen years showed that the numbers of tawny owls and their breeding success in terms of numbers of chicks fledged depended very much on the availability of food and the effects of weather. During incubation the female stays on the nest and is fed by the male, but if the weather is bad and food short the male may not return often enough with sufficient food, and the female may then be forced to leave to do her own hunting. When this happens the eggs may become chilled and fail to hatch. Under normal conditions the eggs hatch at intervals of days so where there are several chicks the first-born is the largest and the last the smallest. If the food supply is insufficient for all the chicks, the largest will get most meals because it is the strongest and the youngest will die. In this way nature ensures that some chicks will survive, whereas if the food were shared equally the whole brood might perish in times of shortage.

During the period of maximum population density, each pair of tawny owls required about twelve hectares for their territory in closed woodland and about twenty in more open woodland. If the pairs had smaller territories, and as little as four hectares has been recorded, then the birds failed to breed. The mean size of territory gradually decreased during the course of the population build-up but the area did not appear to be influenced by the annual fluctuations in the numbers of rodents. This is interesting because here territory size did not appear to b determined primarily by the food supply.

Left: Opossums are typically South American animals, the only one that reaches temperate North America is Didelphis marsupialis, *famous for its habit of feigning death – 'playing possum'. It feeds on insects and small mammals, as well as on fruit and vegetable matter.*

Below: This porcupine may look appealing, but in parts of North America it is a serious pest of plantations as it prefers to feed on the tender cambium layer of young trees.

MAMMALS OF THE FOREST

The mammal fauna of the temperate forest is much less rich in species than the birdlife. Over a thousand different birds are listed in an ornithological field guide covering Europe, while a similar book on mammals includes only 231 species. Of these over thirty are whales, dolphins and porpoises, so that barely two hundred terrestrial mammals are recorded in the vast area north of the Mediterranean and west of the Urals.

As one would expect, most of these species are animals of woodland or woodland edge, survivors of the vast forests which, before the ascent of man, dominated the landscape below the treeline from the Mediterranean shores to the northern tundra. A surprising number either live in trees or else are expert climbers – squirrels, martens, the wild cat, genet, lynx, several rodents and many bats.

In North America there are additional species such as the porcupine, cougar, raccoon and a number of smaller animals. The raccoon has been introduced into one or two parts of Europe, which also has one porcupine, called the crested porcupine. This inhabits part of Italy and is thought to have been introduced by the Romans. The Canadian porcupine is a widespread and common animal and damages trees – particularly conifers, which it prefers – by eating the tender cambium layer directly beneath the bark. It climbs up the trunk, site on one of the whorls of branches and gnaws away at the bark. Sometimes the porcupine will return and enlarge the scar, and occasionally trees are girdled and killed in the process.

The wolf – a history of persecution

The original forests of Europe were soon broken up with the advance of agriculture and the larger mammals, particularly the predators, declined in numbers, and to a greater extent later on when the hunter began to use the percussion-cap cartridge. Effective game laws and the management of forest for limited hunting soon restored the status of the large herbivores such as deer, but the carnivores continued to be destroyed as enemies of man and his interests. None has suffered in this way more than the wolf. Until comparatively recent times it was widely distributed throughout temperate and northern Europe and probably still survives in reasonable numbers in the forests of Siberia and some of the more remote parts of central Europe.

In North America the first European colonists to arrive in the seventeenth century found the wolf – the grey wolf, as it was called – a very abundant and widespread animal. It soon proved to be a nuisance around the new settlements, particularly by preying on domestic stock, and also by interfering with the development of the fur trade. As early as 1630 a bounty of a penny per wolf was paid by the Massachusetts Bay Company in an attempt to control

their numbers. In spite of every man's hand being turned against them, by the middle of the eighteenth century, a hundred years later, wolves were still so numerous that a proposal was made to build a fence across Cape Cod in order to protect the livestock in that area. Elsewhere in North America continuous killing and trapping was beginning to take effect and by 1800 wolves had largely been destroyed in New England and eastern Canada. The last wolf in New England was killed in Maine in 1860, although a few survived in Pennsylvania and upper New York state until the turn of the century: New York paid out six bounties in 1897.

With the slaughter of the bison in the nineteenth century, wolves and their relation the coyote turned their attention to domestic livestock, which were already abundant on the grasslands formerly occupied by the bison. Both the wolf and coyote thrived on the cattle and at least for a time were said to have killed nearly half the calf crop in any year. The cowmen attacked the wolves with traps, bullets and arsenic, but in 1896 the manager of the Standard Cattle Company still complained to the Biological Survey that the 'number of wolves have become so considerable that all means of extermination used in the last five years have only succeeded in keeping them at a standstill.' He thought that the wolf created even more damage than the cattle thieves active at that time and that the cost to the cattlemen was in

the order of a million dollars a year, four times the entire revenue needed to run the State government. Another rancher, in New Mexico, estimated that half a million head of livestock were destroyed annually by the wolves.

It was clear that the bounty system was having no effect and the Biological Survey recommended that wolf dens should be hunted out and the young destroyed. In addition, the rangers in the national forests were authorized to begin widespread trapping operations. The systematic control was organized so that the western ranges were divided into supervised districts and in 1907 the combined efforts of private and federal staff accounted for 1,800 wolves and more than ten times that number of coyotes. Within ten years the wolf problem had been solved, but the last wolves died very hard indeed. Some animals became renowned for avoiding all forms of bait and traps and outwitted the hunters for several years. One old male, called 'Rags the Digger', managed to kill some ten thousand dollars' worth of Colorado stock over a period of fourteen years, while another, 'Old Whitey', was pursued for fifteen years before she was eventually shot by one of the famous wolf hunters of the day. This particular wolf had a five-hundred-dollar bounty on its head, at that time a considerable sum. Today, the last native grey wolves roam in the northern forests of Michigan, Wisconsin, Minnesota and possibly Oregon, but it seems doubt-

Left: The Italian wolf, a small subspecies of Canis lupus *survives in small numbers in the central Apennines. As a result of studies on its biology by Italian scientists, it is now fully protected.*

*Right: The grey wolf (*Canis lupus*) is a true animal of the wilderness, inhabiting both timbered and open areas. In the winter it roams widely in search of food.*

ful whether these scattered bands can survive for very long. A few wolves wander north from Mexico into Arizona and New Mexico and, of course, there are still strongholds in the wilderness areas of western Canada and Alaska.

There is a second species of wolf in North America called the red wolf, somewhat smaller than the grey. It is typically an animal of the southern woodlands and survives today in diminishing numbers in east Texas and western Louisiana, with a few in Oklahoma, Arkansas and southern Missouri. There seems little doubt that it will follow its larger relative into oblivion in the not too distant future.

The destruction of predators can have disastrous consequences in certain situations. In the Kaibab Game Reserve, established in 1906 on the northern rim of the Grand Canyon, Arizona, more than 6000 large predators – mainly wolves, mountain lions, coyotes, bobcats and golden eagles – were systematically eliminated. Free from predation, the deer population increased during the next seventeen years from about 4000 to over 100,000. They rapidly ate up all the available food and the reserve looked as if a swarm of locusts had swept through it, leaving the range torn, grey, stripped and dying. Although the Forest Service staff tried to reduce the population so that the remaining deer had enough to eat, some 60,000 died of starvation. Numbers dwindled to about 10,000 and the ruined rangeland recovered slowly in the following years. A similar story is told of the Isle Royale in Lake Superior, where the numbers of moose rapidly increased after the deliberate extermination of wolves. In this case, however, the wolves later recolonized the island across the winter ice and the ecological balance between wolves, moose and the natural vegetation was eventually restored.

Because the conflict between man and wolf in North America has taken place in comparatively recent times, it has attracted the interest of scientists and a good deal of research on the control of numbers in relation to game animals has been done by American game biologists. In Europe the wolf was eliminated long ago from many areas and at present is virtually extinct in Scandinavia and very local in Spain, while a few are still surviving in the Apennines of central Italy. It is more frequent further east in Russia and also in the Balkans, Greece and Turkey. In England and Wales it was exterminated as early as 1500, in Scotland in about 1740, and in Ireland thirty years later.

The Spanish wolf is a distinct variety, being smaller and paler than the wolf of northern Europe, and is a rather solitary forest animal, surviving in a few regions in the central and western parts of the country. Although it is said to take sheep where they are accessible, generally speaking it makes very little trouble for man and there are few if any well-authenticated cases of it attacking human beings. Neverthe-

less it is regarded as an undesirable animal and is likely to be shot on sight or poisoned. In parts of Spain it also suffers from the activities of the many feral dogs. A few years ago when two children were attacked in a rural area of northern Spain the wolf was blamed and there was a public outcry for its destruction, though responsible opinion believed that the attack was made by a dog which was living wild.

Although it is generally agreed by biologists that the remnants of the wolf populations are declining everywhere in western Europe, and the species may well be extinct by the end of the century, there is some slight change in public opinion in favour of allowing it to survive, at least in areas where it can do so without harm to man. There has also been a change in North America, where restrictions are now put on the ways in which wolves can be hunted. Prior to 1959 there was no limit on the number which could be shot; there was a continuous open season for trapping, wolf dens could be destroyed, and bounties were paid. Even hunting from the air was permitted. After 1959 the bounty system was gradually stopped, wolves were classified as big game and fur-bearers, summer trapping was made illegal and licences were required for the killing of wolves in the non-breeding season. Aerial hunting was stopped in 1972. This programme has helped, because there has been a considerable increase in the wolf population.

The brown bear

Although the future of the wolf in Europe seems to be uncertain, another large forest carnivore, the brown bear, may be holding its own more successfully. It still occurs in Scandinavia, mostly in Sweden, in Finland and of course in Russia, where the greater part of the Old World bear population survives. A few more are found in the Spanish and French Pyrenees, though its future there is uncertain, and a further small population occurs in the mountains of northern Spain. Four or five are said to be extant in the Italian Alps and there is a reasonably healthy population of about a hundred in the Italian Apennines, mainly in the area of the Abruzzo National Park, where every effort is made to protect them.

Further east the brown bear occurs in Czechoslovakia and Poland, especially in the Tatra National Park, where some 300 animals are said to exist. In spite of its large size, it is in fact extremely shy of man and declines in numbers wherever there is too much disturbance in the forest, either by tourists or when roads have to be built for the exploitation of timber. Recent studies have been made in Norway on the relationship between bears and man. Today only small populations survive, but in the middle of the nineteenth century the brown bear was common in most of the forested areas of Norway. In a period of a hundred years up to 1969 a population of

Right: Bear country – the forests of the Abruzzo National Park are still the home of the brown bear. The wise management of this park has helped maintain a healthy population of brown bears.

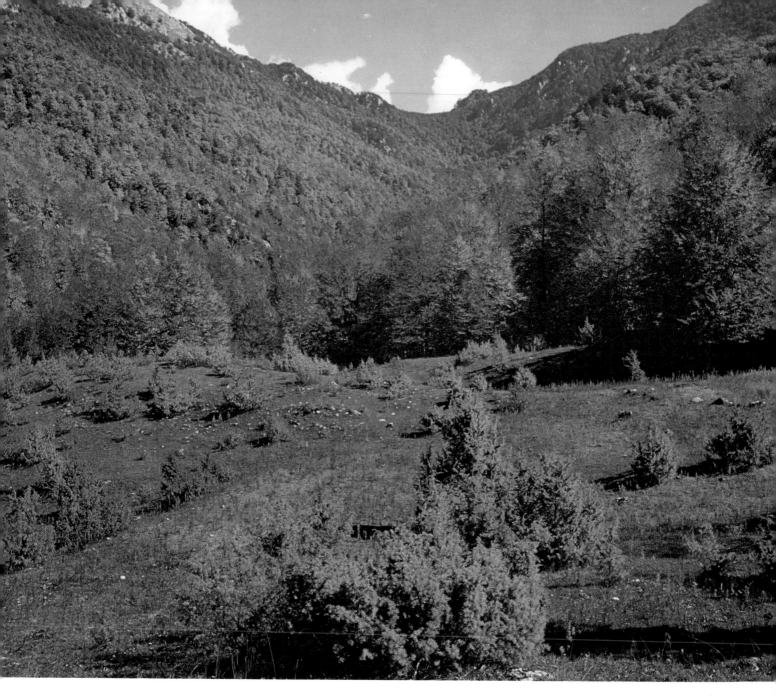

several thousand bears declined to between twenty-five and fifty. Hunting had very little effect on the number of bears because so few were killed, but from about the second half of the 1950s there was a rapid decline which was almost certainly caused by increase in human activity.

The areas most severely influenced by man were the first to be abandoned by bears and the most important factor was the spread of mechanized forestry. Both in the Pyrenees and in Scandinavia it has been shown that there is a direct relationship between the number and length of roads built into the forest and the decline in the number of bears. This type of disturbance causes them to wander much greater distances, breaking up the population groups and making them more vulnerable to destruction by sheep farmers when they enter new territories where their presence is resented.

The same conclusion was reached by Italian biologists in the Abruzzo National Park where forestry operations caused an immediate abandonment of the region by the resident bears. The frequent penetration of the forest by tourists has a similar effect, the most serious aspect being the spread of holiday homes which may be occupied for much of the summer. All these disruptions of the forest environment combine to cut off the traditional migration routes and break up the feeding patterns, which in turn interfere with reproduction.

The most critical period for the bear is the late autumn when it is preparing to make its winter den. At this time it is even more shy and tries to find some part of the forest which is relatively undisturbed. It seems unlikely that the bears in western Europe will expand their population even if protected, and the increased use of State forests by the tourist and forester may drive out the few remaining bears from the areas where they should be allowed to live in peace.

Within the vast territory of the USSR the bear is much more widespread and common, the Russians claiming that two-thirds of the world population of brown bears live in their country. In the republic of Kazakhstan, a large region bordering China, there may be anything from four to thirty-seven bears per thousand hectares. In spring, immediately after leaving the den, these bears spread out along the mountain ridges and migrate to the lower forests where the snow has melted and they can find green vegetation. In the summer they move back into the forest and up into the subalpine and alpine zones in their search for food. In late summer and autumn they return to the lower forest slopes where ripening berries, apples and other fruits are available.

The forest of Kazakhstan consists of mixed fir and cedar with some areas of deciduous trees. There are many berry-carrying bushes and shrubs such as dog rose, honeysuckle, raspberry, currant and bearberry,

which are most important food items of the brown bear in the period prior to hibernation.

In Estonia certain management practices are undertaken specifically for the benefit of bears in an attempt to preserve this small republic's population, which is thought to be not more than 150. The hunters will leave the carcases of animals in the forest as a food supply and in some places oats are sown in clearings and left for the bears to eat. The same type of management is employed in the Abruzzo National Park, where special crops are grown in certain areas so that the bears do not go out of the Park and make a nuisance of themselves on the local farms.

The brown bear hibernates during the winter by excavating a den, often at the roots of a tree, where it remains throughout the cold months of the year. The dens are difficult to find when they are occupied, as the bear camouflages the entrance, but after emergence in spring they are more conspicuous. The area selected for hibernation is of particular importance. In some parts of Asiatic Russia the den is sited on a south-facing slope and is often lined with branches and twigs. If conditions are wet the bears tend to prefer small caves.

Brown bears spend an average of five to six months in their dens, but to some extent this depends on the available food supply. In the mountain pine forests they go to their dens when the first snows come, but in oak forests where there is a rich harvest of acorns hibernation may be delayed. Most bears emerge during April when fresh green vegetation is beginning to show, though there may still be snow on the ground. In the Abruzzo, bears like to graze on grass in the springtime and have been seen together with deer, eating the fresh growth in the open glades of the forest.

The bear's food consists largely of fruit, berries, leaves and insects, mammals making up only about sixteen per cent of the diet. Carrion is also important and bears soon finish off dead animals when they find them. In good years their body weight may increase thirty to thirty-five per cent but in lean years some are not able to hibernate because of insufficient fat and die during the severe winter weather. Others may succeed in going into hibernation but then come out too early and perish. A hungry bear can be a dangerous animal, both to people and to fellow bears. In Baikal, in eastern Siberia, hunters are most frequently attacked during the winter months when the bears are most hungry. In years of shortage they often appear around settlements where they may attack domestic animals. In 1972, in the southern Urals, some 159 head of cattle, 58 head of other livestock and 13 horses were killed.

The female does not breed until she is about four years old and afterwards she will give birth to young every other year. Mating takes place in the middle of May to the beginning of June and the young are born in the early part of the following year while the female is still in the den. Considering the size of the adult bear, the newly-born cubs are very tiny and weigh between 450 and 500 g. When they leave the den they have increased to about two kilograms. Normally there are two cubs in a litter but it may occasionally consist of one or three; four is extremely rare.

The grizzly

In addition to the brown bear, North America has two other species: the grizzly, which earned the scientific name of *Ursus horribilis*, is the largest of the three and is treated with respect by hunters. Although formerly widespread in the United States, grizzlies are now found only in the high mountain country and wilderness areas of the large national parks and forests. Further north, however, in Alaska and west Canada, they are still relatively abundant. Because of their large size they mature rather late and the average female is not able to produce young until she is about five years old. The cubs, usually one or two, are born in the spring or summer and the long weaning period means that the female grizzly cannot produce young more than once in two years; sometimes it may be only once in three or four years. A 25-year-old female – the greatest age so far recorded for a grizzly – could at most have thirteen cubs in her lifetime.

Under natural conditions the grizzly bear's main food is green vegetation, roots and tubers, berries, pine nuts, small rodents and occasionally large herbivores. In the national parks, the bears have learned to forage in the rubbish dumps and in some areas this has been an important source of food. As recently as 1967 it was said that as many as seventy grizzlies could be seen foraging among the refuse of the Trout Creek dump in the Yellowstone National Park. These dumps have now been closed in order to prevent the bears from coming into contact with visitors.

The grizzly, like other large predators, had few natural enemies under primitive conditions and consequently evolved a relatively low reproductive rate. In modern times man has acted as a super-predator

and can inflict heavy mortality in a very short time. When this happens animals such as the grizzly cannot compensate by a rapid increase in reproduction. In fact, effective control measures or excessive hunting can cause a rapid and perhaps irreversible decline in population size. This is probably why the grizzly survives today only in the large national parks and the national forest wilderness areas, where the species is protected from excessive mortality.

The hibernation den usually faces south, with a gallery some two or more metres in length, with a chamber at the end. The chamber is normally higher than the entrance, so that the whole area is freely drained and lined with a bed of vegetation on which to hibernate. During the first two to four weeks of hibernation, the bear's metabolism is much reduced. The heart beat of a sleeping bear slows down from 54 to about 24 per minute, but may even be as low as 8 to 10 beats per minute in older animals. The reduction in body temperature is rather less than one might expect, with a fall of only about five degrees centigrade. The hibernating bear can easily be aroused from its sleep by disturbance and during mild weather may actually emerge for a time, returning again when the weather gets colder. If a hibernating bear is deliberately disturbed its heart beat and temperature rapidly increase, speeding up the utilization of its food reserves. Should this happen repeatedly the bear may suffer by running out of its stored fat before the new spring growth is available.

Conflict between grizzly and man seems inevitable in this modern age, when national parks are increasingly used by large numbers of people. Surprisingly, there are few nasty incidents. For example, in the period 1960–69 there were an

Far right: The black bear is the most common bear of North America. In the east of the country it is black while in the west it tends to be brown or cinnamon-coloured.

Right: A grizzly bear sow with her cubs in Alaska. Arctic shrubs with berries are an important source of food beyond the tree line.

stimated half million visitors to the Yellowstone National Park and only one injury inflicted by grizzly bears was reported. During the same period the Banff National Park in the Canadian Rockies had several million visitors but again only one reported injury, while throughout the whole of North America where grizzly bear populations occur there were twenty-three reported injuries in eighteen separate incidents.

Females with cubs were responsible for three-quarters of these injuries and there is some evidence that old bears are likely to be more dangerous than others. Over half the recorded attacks were on people who had run away at the sight of the bear: the recommendation made to the visitor is to stand still in the hope that the bear will not launch its attack.

The third species of bear in North America, the black bear, is the smallest and, typically, a species of the forest swamps and mountains. It, too, has adapted itself particularly well to the presence of man and its numbers are still at a reasonably high level in much of the original range from Florida and Mexico to Alaska.

Deer

A forest setting would be incomplete without a herd of deer quietly browsing the undergrowth. Deer are in fact widespread throughout the temperate forests of the world, one of the most common being the red deer which in Asia and North America is generally known as the wapiti, or elk (a name given to the moose in Europe). Some authorities believe that this is a distinct species because obvious differences can be seen, but others, and perhaps the majority, consider that there is only one species with different geographical forms in various parts of the world. If we accept the view that there is only one species, there are some sixteen described subspecies which can be identified.

Throughout Europe there is considerable variation in size. For example, the red deer of Scotland are small and somewhat unimpressive animals, whereas the red deer of Hungary, Yugoslavia and Bulgaria are about two to two-and-a-half times as heavy and the antler weight is three to four times greater than those found on the Scottish hills. The wapiti of Asia and North America are also appreciably larger.

The maximum life-span of the red deer is about twenty years; they breed only once each year, with the mating season in late autumn. Pregnancy extends throughout the winter and the calves are born in early summer, usually late May to late June. The males live apart from the females and young for much of the year and in the rutting season challenge each other for the hinds, which they collect together in groups and defend against other males. In Britain the main red deer population of about 270,000 is on the hill-land of Scotland.

Although popular as a sport animal, it is also useful for the production of venison and some biologists believe that this is the best way to utilize the poor-quality hill-land which extends over such a vast area of Scotland. The annual deer cull amounts to somewhere between twenty-five and thirty thousand animals, which is equivalent to a thousand metric tons of dressed carcases. Venison is not a popular meat in Britain but is highly prized in Germany, which imports most of the Scottish animals. In North America, trading in venison is illegal in order to discourage poaching, but the meat is much valued by the private hunters, who are able to use the animals they shoot. Over much of Europe hunting rights are associated with land tenure, but in North America game is State-owned so that there are common hunting rights which can be licensed to the hunter by the State. This has certain advantages because the State is able to use some of the income for research on range and forest management for game animals. In Europe hunting is very much orientated to obtaining the best trophies. The antlers are assessed in terms of measurement and weight, and the cost to the hunter varies accordingly, with the best trophies being the most expensive.

Although red deer is predominantly a woodland animal, a common feature of the forest habitat where it occurs is the presence of grassy clearings, fields and forest rides within and adjacent to the woods. The European red deer rarely penetrates into the large dense forest but prefers more open areas. This association with woodland edge, where the woodland passes into grassland, is also found in countries where the red deer has been introduced. In Australia, for instance, they occur in large numbers where there are cleared grassy slopes, open forest and where forest scrub, grassland or open mountain lie in close proximity.

The red deer eats a wide variety of different plants with grasses forming the greater proportion of the food taken, although elsewhere shrub or tree foliage may be particularly important items of the diet. Red deer in Scotland do not do much damage to timber because they live away from the main commercial forest, but there are records of them feeding readily in cornfields, meadows, pastures and in arable crops, especially when other food is scarce. There are several examples in North America of excessive deer populations causing great changes to the vegetation cover and two incidents have been described earlier.

The wapiti does not appear to cause such great

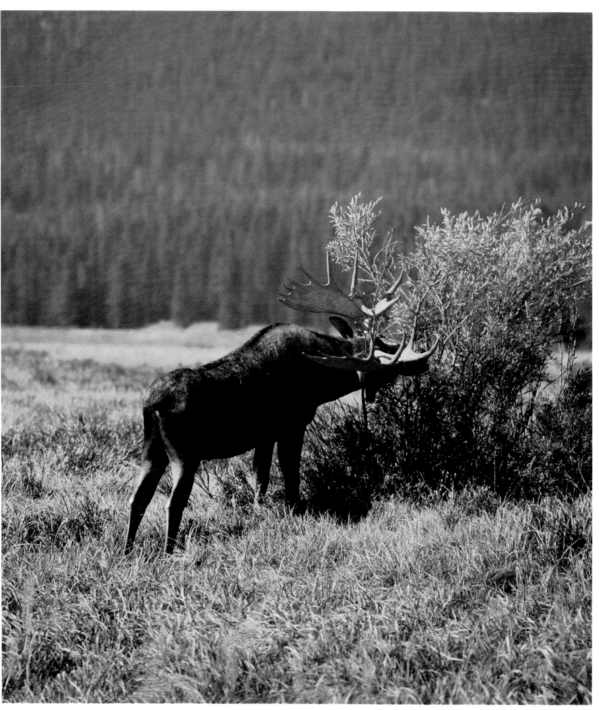

Left: Although the moose is found across the northern coniferous belt, its behaviour seems to differ according to its location. In Sweden and northern Russia it is thriving and seems to prefer forests that lie close to cultivated land, while in North America the moose still clings to true forest wilderness and as a result has retreated northwards and declined in numbers.

Right: Domestic reindeer being herded into an enclosure in Finland. Wild reindeer are no longer found in the Old World but in North America large herds of the closely related caribou still survive.

problems, perhaps because the range biologists have done a good deal of research into the carrying capacity of the forest areas. Where damage does occur it is usually from browsing on the foliage or gnawing the bark of trees. On the whole, broadleaved trees such as willows, poplars, oak and ash are preferred, but the red deer will also take juniper and species of pine and spruce. Bark stripping may be widespread, particularly in central and eastern Europe. Generally the younger trees between seven and twenty years suffer the heaviest damage, and in some cases the tree or branch may be completely girdled and killed. Both broadleaved trees, such as poplars and beech, and many species of conifers are also damaged. The bark seems to be most attractive in spring, when the sap is rising and it can more easily be peeled off the main stem. Winter damage is also widespread but at that time the bark is more difficult to remove and the deer usually have to gnaw it off with their incisor teeth.

The much smaller roe deer is also a favourite game animal. More widely distributed than the red deer, it is able to maintain itself successfully in small lowland woods in areas where there is intensive agriculture. On the Kalø estate in Denmark the roe deer population fluctuates around the hundred mark on an area of 630 hectares, of which 400 hectares is forest. Here the deer make good use of both forest and surrounding agricultural crops. Forest is essential for cover and breeding, while in winter the grass fields and root crops are a favourite source of food. In early summer the roe deer feed in the beech forest, where they are particularly fond of the rhizomes,

leaves and flowers of the wood anemone. In late summer, autumn and early winter, clover and grass become important, followed by root crops, though the adjacent woodland is always important as a retreat in time of danger.

The roe deer reaches its full size at about sixteen months when the males stand at about 64–67 cm and the females slightly less. The average weight of the adult male is 26 kg and that of the female about two kilograms lighter. Their antlers are shed each year and are quite small, never exceeding more than about 30 cm. Each antler normally has three points, but size and shape often vary even in the same animal from one year to the next. As they grow older the animals tend to lose weight and the condition and quality of the antlers decline. Nevertheless, age and experience seem to be the most important criteria in defence of territory, and the younger males are less aggressive, tending to emigrate to new areas rather than fight it out with the males who have already held territory.

Rutting takes place from mid-July to mid-August and the female can bear young as early as the second year. The roe deer differs from other species of deer in that after fertilization the egg develops for a short while and then remains free in the uterus from August until December or January, when rapid development and implantation take place. About seventy per cent of the adult females produce two fawns, and triplets are also known. The speckled fawns can walk within a few hours of birth, but are usually left hidden in the vegetation until they have grown appreciably. By two to three months of age they

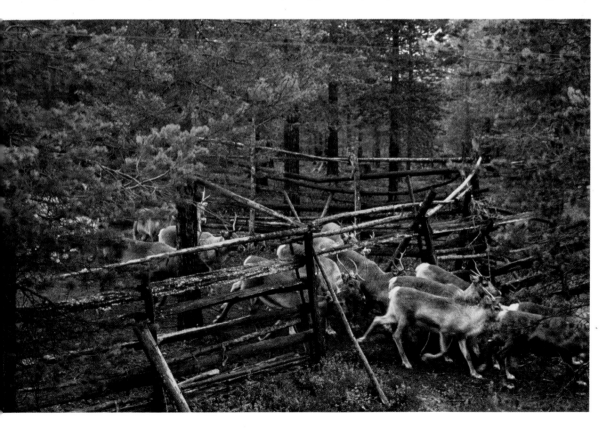

follow their mothers and remain with them.

A number of other small deer can be seen in European woodlands, although they may originally have come from other parts of the world. For example, the muntjac and the Chinese water deer are now widespread in woodlands in England, having escaped from zoological parks where they were kept in captivity. Fallow deer and sika have also established themselves from park escapes, although the former was probably introduced to Britain many years ago, probably by the Romans, and subsequently on other occasions. The sika deer is a native of the Japanese islands and Taiwan, and countries on the continent of Asia within the eastern Palaearctic region. Herds have been established in parks all over Europe and animals which escape have colonized many woodland areas. It is very similar to the red deer but smaller in size, with rows of pale spots on the pelage.

The familiar reindeer of Scandinavia is not a forest animal but its close relative in North America, the woodland caribou, can be found throughout the mixed deciduous forests of Quebec, Ontario, Manitoba, Saskatchewan, Alberta and the North-west Territories. Like so many of the larger forest animals of North America it was formerly much more widespread, extending from Vermont in the United States to Nova Scotia in east Canada and west to British Columbia. The total population today is probably somewhere between fourteen and fifteen thousand and it must be regarded almost as an endangered species in North America. The European reindeer was introduced as a domestic animal into arctic Canada to provide an easy food supply for the Eskimos, but this experiment was not successful because it is not part of the Eskimos' tradition to domesticate animals, and the reindeer have now mostly dispersed and gone wild.

The caribou of North America are the largest of the races of reindeer which have been described throughout the world. They differ from other members of the deer family in that both sexes possess antlers, although the male's are larger and rather more complex. They appear to be clumsily-built animals, with large hooves and hairy muzzles not found in other species of the deer family. Their coat is compact and dense, clove-brown in colour above and white beneath, with a white tail patch. The ears and tail are short and the throat has a deep mane.

The woodland caribou browse on the foliage of trees, and on the islands of Lake Superior the mountain maple is the principal local food. The ground-living reindeer mosses are, of course, eaten and also lichens growing on trees. In spring the caribou excavate roots and shoots of herbs with their hooves, and get at the moss and lichens beneath the snow. They are mainly browsers during the summer but also eat aquatic plants growing in the woodland waterways.

Right: The fallow deer is a handsome animal with a spotted coat and palmate antlers. Originally native to the Mediterranean region and Middle East, it has been introduced into many parts of western Europe.

Left: The roe deer is small, fast and graceful It inhabits mixed woodland and forest an open areas with a good cover of bushes.

The fox and the badger

The European fox and badger are two of the best known medium-sized woodland animals, probably because they feature in children's stories more often than any other animal apart from the rabbit. The fox and the rabbit are traditionally linked as predator and prey, but the former can do without the latter, as indeed it had to during the 1950s and 1960s, when all but a few rabbits were killed off by myxomatosis.

The fox is distributed throughout Europe from Spain to arctic Scandinavia and there are several other species elsewhere in Asia and North America, including the small arctic fox. In Britain the fox is a native animal, whose remains can be traced back for many thousands of years. On the other hand, the rabbit was introduced in the twelfth century and did not become common until the seventeenth and eighteenth centuries when the warrens where they were artificially reared were ploughed up and many

rabbits escaped into the sorrounding countryside. I lowland regions the rabbit prefers the woodlan edge, seeking cover and shelter under the trees, bu generally feeding is out in the open. But it is wide spread and common in many areas devoid of tree particularly in the uplands and on open heathland.

The fox, too, is highly versatile, but away from the upland area it prefers to live in woodland o scrub. Its ability to survive in Europe in spite of bein branded as a pest is a remarkable tribute to the fox' resilience and adaptability. The popularity of fox hunting during recent centuries has undoubtedl helped, and in many parts of Britain its number have been maintained because scrubby woodland areas known as fox coverts have been provided for i to breed in peace, and to make it easier for the hun ters to find their quarry. As this sport declines, with the present period of much more intensive agricul ture, the increasing number of nature reserves ar oviding a refuge for this interesting animal.

On the continent of Europe the fox has been having a difficult time recently because it is a carrier of the dangerous disease of rabies. This is easily transmitted to dogs with the consequent risk to people who might be bitten. The disease is usually fatal to fox, dog and man alike, although vaccination has greatly helped to save human lives. Rabies control in many European countries has consisted of intensive campaigns to destroy the fox populations in regions where the disease has been reported. Britain has been free from the disease for more than fifty years, mainly because of the strict control exercised over the importation of live animals, particularly dogs.

The badger has also been implicated in spreading disease – tuberculosis – by infecting cattle grazing in the fields where the badgers go in search of dung-beetles in the cowpats. Occurrences have been very

localized in south-west Britain and on practically every other count the badger must be regarded as a harmless or even beneficial animal. It seldom takes game or domestic stock or poultry and, although it feeds on a very wide variety of plant and animal food, it seems to prefer earthworms, which form the bulk of its diet. During the day it lies in its sett, or burrow, in a chamber lined with plant material such as bracken which makes a warm and comfortable bed. About dusk it emerges and follows regular pathways which are often conspicuous because they are so well trodden. The badger has a curious ambling gait with the broad hindquarters swaying from side to side. Its track is very easy to recognize and resembles that of a small bear. The five toe pads lie close together, the five claws extending a little way in front. The broad main pad is also very characteristic. In commercial forests badgers are welcomed because they excavate and destroy the nest of bees and wasps, having a special liking for honey and the larvae of these insects. Another useful rôle, this time to the farmer's benefit, is the destruction of rabbit nests. The badger is too slow to catch adult rabbits but they are efficient at detecting and digging out the covered-over burrows containing young rabbits.

The rabbit, fox and badger are successful animals because they are generalized in their food preferences and way of life. They can adapt to many different environments, are able to turn to alternative food sources if their favourites become unavailable, and they will breed happily in close proximity with man as well as in much more remote areas.

Above: The European badger is a favourite of wildlife enthusiasts. It is a nocturnal, social mammal, feeding on a wide range of animal and plant food.

Left: In spite of intensive persecution throughout Europe, the red fox manages to hold its own. In England the fox is quite commonly found in suburban gardens and on derelict waste ground of inner cities. On the continent it carries rabies and is destroyed at every opportunity.

The demand for fur

It is not possible to describe all the smaller forest mammals of the temperate regions but some mention should be made of those which were so important to the fur trade. The development of a thick fur is an adaptation to the bitterly cold winters of the northern latitudes and dark coniferous forests of North America, Europe and Siberia; a cold climate encourages a rich coat of fur, the wet habitat increases its lustre, while the woodland shade protects the dark sheen from the bleaching effects of the sunlight. The most precious fur-bearers were various members of the weasel family, of which perhaps the stoat or ermine is one of the best known. But others which were more important from an economic point of view are the otter, mink, pine marten, fisher and wolverine. Even the striped skunk, another member of the weasel family, became important for its fur when the more favoured species began to decline.

The larger of the chief fur-bearers, the marten, fisher and wolverine, are fierce solitary carnivores which depend on deep unbroken tracts of virgin forest. Some, such as the wolverine, were probably never very common south of the Canadian border, while the others have declined considerably due to hunting pressure. The fisher is a relatively large ani-mal and its pelt fetched as much as 345 dollars, a pric which has undoubtedly contributed to its decline. has also suffered from forest exploitation, fires, an the elimination of pregnant females during wint trapping. Unlike the wolverine and the marten, th fisher is not widespread in Alaska and is still trappe wherever it is found. But its chief peril may be th lumbermen who destroy the bark-eating porcupin an important source of food.

Bring back the beaver

Perhaps the best known and most popular of th fur-bearing animals is the beaver. In North Ameri it was extremely abundant throughout most of th continent where there were forests. But when th early European colonists found that the fur was excellent for winter clothing it was widely exploite and started to decline even as early as 1638, when had the misfortune to be in demand for the manu facture of hats. In the first half of the nineteen century it had disappeared in the Atlantic and wester states of America and was declining elsewhere at rapid rate. The beaver hat went out of fashion at th beginning of the nineteenth century but short afterwards the beaver itself virtually became extin east of the Mississippi.

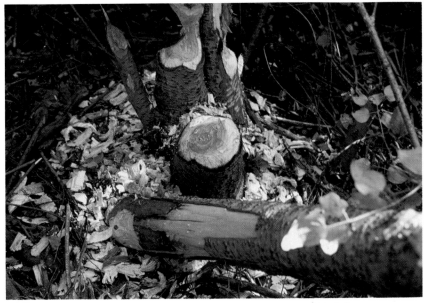

The beaver was also formerly widespread throughout the whole of western Europe, though today it is found in very few places. Even in Britain it seems to have been common in post-glacial times and fossil remains of its bones are known from many places, particularly in East Anglia. In recent years a number of reintroductions have been made in Europe, notably in Sweden, Finland and Switzerland. The most recent of these have been successful and the Swiss are now thinking of reintroducing it to other parts of their country. It has been equally successful in Sweden, where it is increasing and spreading in many areas, causing some forestry problems, particularly with regard to timber transport. Lumbermen find they have to destroy the beavers' dams when the waterways are obstructed and the logs cannot be floated down stream.

Even in Russia the beaver had become scarce by the beginning of the twentieth century and only a few hundred remained in European Russia and western Siberia. In the 1920s national parks were created to protect it and the population rapidly increased. The most important area was the Voroniez National Park, from which 700 beavers were moved to other localities between 1934 and 1947. During the last thirty years about nine-and-a-half thousand beavers have been successfully moved to other forest areas to start up new colonies, and as a result of protection and management there are now between forty-five and fifty thousand beavers in the USSR. By 1963 the population had reached a level at which it was possible to start taking an annual crop for the fur trade. The flesh of the beaver does not appear to have been very popular in Europe, although in North America it was acceptable on fast days because it was an aquatic animal.

In Canada, where the beaver is widespread, it depends for food very largely on the inner bark, twigs and leaves of poplars and willows, especially aspens. The trees which are cut down vary widely in size, though they are not often larger than 20 cm in diameter. The upper teeth are dug into the wood and then the beaver chisels away with the lower teeth, working its way round the trunk. In summer it also feeds on aquatic plants of various sorts. As winter approaches the beaver cuts down a large number of logs which he floats into his winter lodge and stores under the water to provide fresh food.

Right: Vermillion Lake and Mount Ridley in the Banff National Park, Alberta, Canada. This famous park is home of mule deer, wapiti, moose, grizzly and black bear.

Below: A close-up of a large beaver showing the coarse hairs of the pelage, which protect the fine inner coat. Until recently the latter was used to make the beaver hats of the Guards' uniform in Britain.

The smaller predators

The modification of such woodland for commercial forestry, its fragmentation into smaller units and the activities of gamekeepers have all contributed to the decline in medium-sized mammal predators in European forests. Polecat, pine marten and wild cat were destroyed at every opportunity but during the last thirty years, as the number of gamekeepers has declined and foresters have become more tolerant and interested in wildlife, these predators have made a recovery. With the growth of public interest in wildlife conservation there has also been a new demand from visitors to forest nature reserves to see such animals as these, which are large enough to be exciting and yet are in no sense dangerous.

The pine marten, which has closely related species in Siberia and North America, is a particularly attractive animal, with a pale throat patch on a rich brown fur, and a bushy tail. The beech or stone marten has a more southerly distribution in Europe, overlapping with the pine marten but generally less confined to wooded areas. Martens are agile climbers and can run fast over short distances on the ground. Their nest is built in a rocky crevice, tree hole or hole in an earth bank, and sometimes they take over the nest of a squirrel or an owl. In Scandinavia the main prey of the pine marten is the red squirrel, but elsewhere in Europe the diet may include voles, birds, eggs, insects and berries.

The polecat and wild cat can live successfully in open country away from forests and the former is often associated with farm buildings and the edges of settlements. In Britain the polecat is found only in Wales and the Welsh border country, while the wild cat is almost entirely confined to Scotland, so the two species do not overlap. The wild cat also lives on the Scottish grouse moors, though it is better established in the forest areas. It is essentially a ground hunter taking hares, rabbits, voles, mice and some birds.

In Spain and western France there is a small cat-like animal called the genet, a nocturnal and shy creature of the denser forests, especially where there are rocky outcrops and streams. This curious creature is related to the mongoose and with its short legs and

Right: The pine marten is an alert and agile forest predator. It feeds on rodents and small birds.

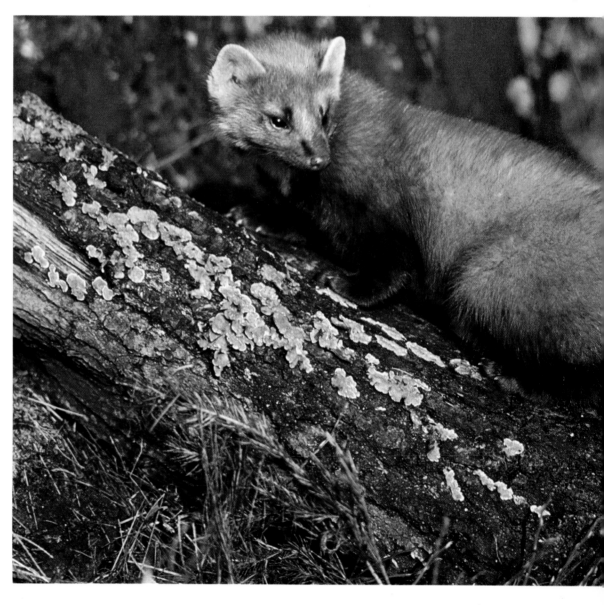

ong body is similar in appearance. The snout is pointed and the long bushy tail is banded, while here are a series of dark spots on the paler fur of the body. Although about the size of a domestic cat, its kin was much prized among country people in the Pyrenees. Many would be trapped during the winter when the villagers had to go into the forest to cut wood, but in recent years as the standard of living as improved, paraffin has replaced wood for heating nd the genet and other fur-bearing animals have been left in peace.

Squirrels

As forest predators tend to be secretive and mainly nocturnal they are generally difficult to see, but the reverse is true for the commoner squirrels. The red squirrel and the American grey squirrel are both diurnal and readily tolerate the presence of man. The former is widespread throughout Europe and Asia, although there are a number of different colour forms. It is primarily a coniferous forest animal, eating the seeds of pine, but will also live in deciduous

woodland if there are no competitors. In Britain it was widespread in many types of woodland before the introduction of the American grey squirrel in the late nineteenth and early twentieth century. In its native habitat the grey prefers dense hardwood forests, particularly oak, hickory and walnut, but also occurs at the southern edge of the conifer belt. When it arrived in Britain it soon established strong populations in deciduous woodland, taking over many areas formerly occupied by the red squirrel, which was then in decline. North America also has a species of red squirrel, but the grey is larger and highly prized as a food and game animal. In Britain, the grey squirrel is regarded by the forester and gamekeeper as a pest and is destroyed whenever possible. In fact many people erroneously believe that it is related to the rats rather than the squirrels and this is a good enough reason to kill it. However, it has been clever enough to establish itself in parks and gardens where it gives a good deal of pleasure to visitors and will often feed from the hand. Neither the red nor the grey have a true hibernation period in Europe and can be seen searching for food on mild winter days. It is at this time that they can cause damage to trees, mainly by stripping off bark from the leader shoots. But their diet is very varied – nuts, seeds, buds, pollen from cones and catkins, berries, roots, bulbs, tubers and even fungi. The grey will also take the eggs and young of woodland birds.

Above: The red squirrel Tamiasciurus hudsonicus *from North America can be distinguished from its relatives by its creamy-white underparts. Squirrels of the northern forests occasionally migrate in large numbers in search of food. This species is active during the day and on moonlit nights. It is not a true hibernator.*

THE FOREST TODAY

Throughout his long history Man seldom adapted himself to the forest as a home and the few tribes known today as inhabitants of tropical forests are exceptions to the main course of evolution. In Africa, where human origins can be traced back in time further than elsewhere, our earliest ancestors probably lived in the open savanna by the forest edge or, as some believe, along the shores of lakes. The forest itself was regarded with a certain amount of fear, because of the enemies and predatory animals it sheltered. For centuries, therefore, Man's energies were devoted mainly to pushing back the limits of the forest to create more land for cultivation and more grassland for grazing, but retaining sufficient woodland for sport, for the herds of swine which dug for roots and ate the acorn crop, and to perpetuate the many types of timber needed in everyday life. Gradually the forest became fragmented into smaller units and the species of trees in them were selected according to their value and use, while the others disappeared or survived only in marginal areas.

In historical times our exploitation of the forest was often motivated by greed and desire for quick profits. We have already seen that in the early days of colonial America the European immigrants recklessly exploited the virgin forests, partly to increase the farmland and partly because they thought that in so vast a country trees were inexhaustible. As in the case of the disappearing buffalo, they came to believe that there were always more 'out west'. Throughout the world the misuse of axe and saw, fire and over-grazing destroyed the forest and led to the disruption of watersheds, erosion and loss of soil fertility, flooding and blocking of waterways with silt. This story has been repeated time and time again, yet the process still goes on, particularly in undeveloped tropical countries where virgin forest areas are unexploited and the lessons of conservation have not yet been learned.

It is only in comparatively recent times that scientists have been able to demonstrate the many dramatic changes which may take place when the protective cover of trees is removed, particularly in regions of high rainfall. Trees not only provide many materials essential to man but they protect and enrich the soil, retain moisture in the ground and act as windbreaks in open country, preventing the dry soil from blowing away. In the mountains they are a natural break to avalanches which otherwise might cause havoc in the human settlements below.

The main characteristic of trees compared with most other plants is that they are long-lived. Not only do they add to their store of organic material year by year but they preserve within the forest an enormous 'bank' of potentially valuable products. This means that man must learn the science of wise management in order to produce a sustained yield, ensuring that the crop taken each year is roughly

Left: Canada still has enormous areas of natural forest but this resource is increasingly feeling the pressures of greater demands from countries with poor timber stock.

Below: Clear felling in the Siuslaw National Forest of Oregon, USA.

equivalent to the increment which is added in the form of new growth. Throughout the world it has been estimated that there are approximately 3,800 million hectares of forest of all kinds. This includes all natural forest, scrubland and savanna with scattered trees. Some sixty per cent of the world's total forest area is productive in the commercial sense, and the total area exploited increases year by year. Much of this is what has been termed forest 'mining', that is, clear-felling, after which the land is left for a secondary forest to grow up, or it is reclaimed for cultivation or grazing. Much of the cut timber is used unwisely: it is estimated that nearly 45 per cent of all trees felled end up as firewood, and in some of the less developed countries it may be as much as 80 per cent. The local people have no alternative fuel in such remote rural areas, and so the finest quality timber may heat the cooking pot or provide material for chicken coops.

FIRST STEPS IN FOREST PROTECTION

Attempts to arrest the wanton exploitation of timber in the United States started in 1891 when the first federal lands were set aside as forest reserves. With the election of Theodore Roosevelt as President the process gathered momentum and by the end of his term of office there were more than sixty-one million hectares being managed as national forests. The

Below: The ravages of ruthless forest exploitation. Here, in New Zealand, a native forest of southern beech has been clear-felled and burned.

orest service programme was based on three main bjectives. The first was to maintain a sustained ield, a policy which has to be related to the growth ate of the tree – a single generation of long-lived iant sequoias might extend over a thousand years r more. Commercial forestry therefore tends to ncourage the planting or selection of fast-growing rees which can be harvested more frequently and so roduce greater profit. Secondly, the forest service ried to follow the principle of multiple use, catering or as many interests as possible – grazing, the preser- ation of wildlife, hunting, outdoor recreation and oil and watershed conservation. Thirdly, the forest ervice was to establish a policy which provided 'the

greatest good for the greatest number' with the emphasis placed first on maintaining the continuity of trees and avoiding the short-term high profit philosophy which has influenced so many other activities. As the population of North America grew, and the demand on forest resources increased, many industrial concerns resented these restrictions and pressure mounted to get the national forests into what they termed full production. Essentially this meant the harvesting of the remaining old-growth timber so that it could be replaced with quicker- growing species. This point of view aimed at pro- moting the commercial aspects of forestry with less consideration given to the multiple-use concept. In 1970 a National Timber Supply Bill was introduced in Congress which would have established timber production as the primary use over the forty million hectares of national forest land. Conservation organ- izations opposed the bill and it was not passed.

Above: A grove of giant sequoias in California. These trees would have ended their days at the saw mill if conservationists had not intervened.

This conflict between commercial activities and the conservation of forest resources continues to the present day, although it is fortunately much less frequent. In the early part of 1978 strong opposition developed to a proposal to extend the National Redwood Park of giant sequoias in California. Someone, fearing that this would cut into the rich profits of the logging industry, severely damaged the once majestic three-thousand-year-old 'Avenue of Giants', which were scarred with deep gashes from a chain saw. Ten trees were completely killed in a series of night raids and eight others are unlikely to survive, having been girdled by the chain saw so as to sever the thin life-supporting layer of sapwood.

FELLING THE GIANTS

This attack is particularly tragic because only about thirteen per cent has survived. The genus *Sequoia* was once common and widespread throughout North America and the Old World, but only one species is known today – the coast redwood *S. sempervirens*. This species holds the record for the tallest tree, the specimen known as 'Howard Libbey' reaching a height of 112.4 m. The closely related *Sequoiadendron gigantea*, known as the 'Big Tree', 'Giant Sequoia', or 'Wellingtonia', may also exceed a hundred metres, and specimens as old as 3,400 years have been recorded. Both these trees survive only in the coastal mountains of California and just into Oregon,

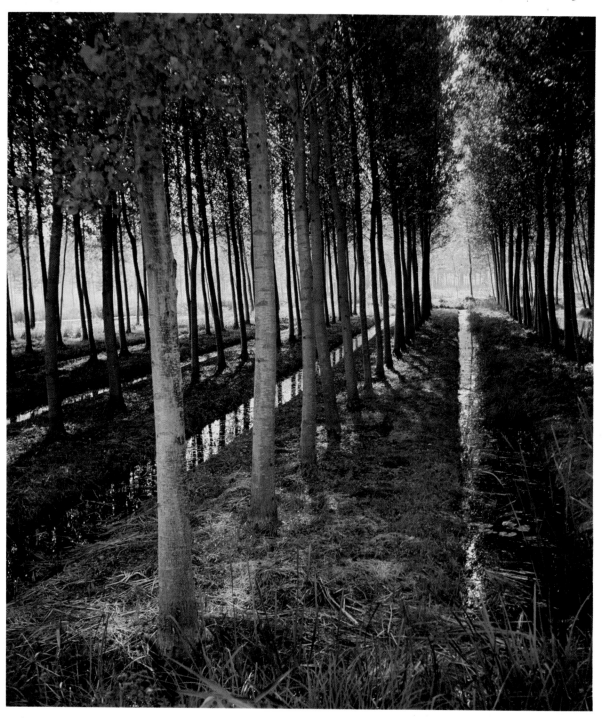

Left: Poplar hybrids are planted in many parts of Europe, especially on waterlogged ground where other crops cannot be grown. These trees grow very rapidly and can be harvested when 15 to 20 years old.

where the ground never freezes and moisture and sunshine abound, providing just the right conditions for a rich variety of conifers. John Muir, who was eloquent in defence of the sequoia at the end of the last century, wrote in 1901: 'Who of all the dwellers of the plains and prairies and fertile home forests of round-headed oak and maple, hickory and elm, ever dreamed that earth would bear such growths – trees that the familiar pines and firs seem to know nothing about, lonely, silent, serene, with a physiognomy almost godlike; and so old, thousands of them still living had already counted their years by tens of centuries when Columbus set sail from Spain and were in the vigor of youth or middle age when the star led the Chaldean sages to the infant Saviour's cradle.' This passage echoes the inspiration and awe felt by so many who have seen these trees and the majesty and friendliness of the sequoias makes the recent vandalism all the more difficult to tolerate, inspiring a devotion to conservation.

The European scene

In Europe, Man established some sort of equilibrium with forests at a much earlier stage, even though this was achieved after much of the forest land had been destroyed. Today only about twenty-nine per cent has forest cover, and most of this is in Scandinavia. In Great Britain, for instance, only about eight per cent of the land now bears trees. On the continent of Europe the situation is rather better, with between twenty and thirty per cent in most of the western countries. Although the total forested area of Europe is only one fifth that of North America, production is nearly four times greater. This difference is almost certainly due to the intensity of skill in management which has developed over the centuries and to the conversion of so many of the native forests to monocultures of quick-growing trees which can be harvested and clear-felled before the land is replanted.

This highly artificial system of forest management has now been found to result in decreasing yields and German foresters have realized that it is better in the long run to adopt a management regime closer to that of a natural woodland. A greater range of tree species have been planted and instead of clear-felling the cropping is now done by selective cutting in order to maintain continuous tree cover. In Switzerland most forest land belongs to the cantons but the federal law also applies to all private owners. Clear-cutting is not allowed, nor can forest land be converted to other uses without federal permission.

Some forest practices may have significant influences on air and water quality. For instance, management may require regular burning in order to eliminate under-brush, control insects and disease, and to create clearings for game. This practice is also intended to get rid of the slash, the branches left after logging, which tend to accumulate and create severe fire risk. Burning will probably decline in the future

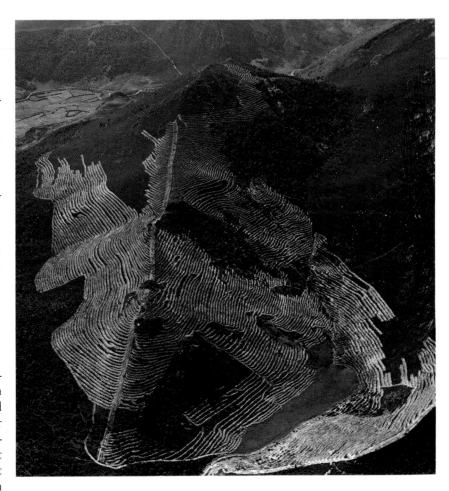

because factories can now take the slash for pulp and chipboard.

Forest streams and their fish populations are also affected by silvicultural activities. Logging and the building of roads damages the stream banks and allows sediments to clog the waterways, debris can impede water-flow and the loss of tree cover changes the normal stream temperature both in winter and summer. Pesticides and fertilizers in areas of intensive forest management may also cause pollution. But all these can be limited by good forest management. For example, buffer zones of trees can be left uncut along the stream borders.

Forested upland areas have for long been regarded as water-collecting grounds which regulate the flow moving through the ground into rivers and lakes. Water catchment areas are therefore often planted with trees and every effort is made to protect them from destructive forces such as fire and avalanche. The large quantity of plant material present in the forest acts as a kind of reservoir, intercepting and holding back precipitation. After heavy rain the flow of water from woodlands is released slowly compared with treeless areas, where there may be sudden flash floods. This reduces erosion and the loss of surface soil. As rain falls on the tree canopy it slowly percolates through to the leaf litter and the soil. This not only slows down the rate to run off but acts as a filter so the water which emerges is of rela-

Above: The creation of a new forest in Spain. The narrow terraces made for the young trees show up as conspicuous scars but these will disappear as the trees grow.

tively high quality, free from sediment and chemicals which often contaminate the water run-off from agricultural land.

Air pollution has now become a major problem in many industrialized countries, mainly because of the effect of sulphur dioxide on the vegetation. Large quantities of this gas originate from smelting works, factories and domestic coal fires and when it dissolves in rain it produces a dilute sulphuric acid which causes the damage. Trees vary in their sensitivity to the effects of sulphur dioxide: the valuable collection of pine trees in the British National Pinetum had to be moved from Kew near London to an area in Kent because of the urban air pollution.

In Canada it has been shown that the white pine is particularly sensitive, young trees failing to appear on plots thirty miles away from the industrial complex responsible for the emission. One of the best-known examples of this effect comes from Copper Hill, Tennessee. Early in the century, the fumes from this smelting works laid waste an area of 7,000 hectares and damaged another 12,500 hectares of hardwood timber.

Even today much of this land is virtually bare and suffering from severe erosion. In Sweden it is believed that the maximum monthly level of sulphur dioxide in the air should not exceed 135 μg/m^3. Coniferous trees are more sensitive to sulphur dioxide than deciduous and may be influ-

enced by levels as low as 56 μg/m^3. In the Ruhr area of northern Germany coniferous trees fail to grow if the levels exceed 196 μg/m^3. Comparable figures for what is regarded as the natural atmospheric levels of sulphur dioxide range from 0.28 to 2.8 μg/m^3.

LICHENS: POLLUTION INDICATORS

A good deal of work has been done in recent years on sensitive plants which are good indicators of aerial pollution. The primitive group called lichens has been shown to be particularly important in this respect. Lichens are very unusual because they do not consist of a single group of living things but are composed of two quite different organisms, a fungus and an alga, which behave as a single biological unit.

Below left: Although many lichens cannot tolerate sulphur dioxide in polluted air, a few such as Leanora conizaeoides *are able to do so.*

Below: Usnea intexta *is one of the beard lichens and consists of tufts of filaments which grow on the bark of trees – in this case oak.* Usnea *species are intolerant to air pollution.*

They are extremely successful plants, occurring all over the world and particularly widespread as symbiotic organisms growing on the bark of trees. Their growth rate is very slow and consequently they live for a long time: some are known to be several centuries old. A lichen growing in Greenland is claimed to be as much as 4,500 years. The chemical nature and texture of the surface on which they grow are important limiting factors, with the result that a single large tree may support several different assemblages of lichen species according to the conditions prevailing in each microhabitat. The acidity of the bark of the tree appears to be particularly important: birch and pine bark are more acid than oak, and so tend to support communities adapted to these conditions. Lichens react sharply to aerial pollution, either by failing to grow or by actually dying if the bark acidity becomes too high; or more tolerant species take over. In industrial areas the lichens growing on the side facing the prevailing winds are the first to decline or disappear.

The dilute sulphuric acid is taken up by the live fronds of the lichen. It accumulates and eventually disrupts the photosynthetic processes by destroying the chlorophyll. Photosynthesis is controlled by the algal component of the lichen and damage is most severe if conditions are moist and there is already a tendency to acidity in the substrate on which it is growing.

Trees and lichens are affected by other airborne pollutants, such fluorides from aluminium smelting works and from brickworks, but in places like Los Angeles and Tokyo the photochemical smog that develops where there is intense motor traffic does not appear to have the same deleterious effect.

During recent years attempts to reduce air pollution in various parts of Europe have met with a degree of success, the emission of sulphur dioxide in urban areas of Britain having fallen considerably since 1958. One of the ways this has been achieved has been by ensuring that industrial chimneys are high enough for the smoke to be carried away from urban areas and dispersed in the upper parts of the atmosphere; this helps to keep the towns cleaner but the pollutant material drifts over much greater distances, and there are now convincing statistics to show that industrial smoke from the Ruhr area of Germany and industrial regions of Britain reach Scandinavia. These pollutants have been shown to be responsible for the increasing acidity in the rain which falls on Swedish forests, causing a reduction in tree growth.

Lichens are not only good watchdogs for the onset of unacceptable levels of aerial pollution, warning the forester and conservationist of what may be taking place, but a well-formed cover of lichens on the bark of a tree is also an important microhabitat for many invertebrate animals. If this growth is completely destroyed, the fauna is lost with it. We know,

for instance, that twenty-seven European moths are dependent on lichens for food, or else rely on them for camouflage when they are resting on the tree trunk. Many other small creatures have also evolved a colouration which is cryptic when they are resting on tree-growing lichens. For instance, the large and handsome black-and-white crab spider, *Philodromus emerginatus*, merges perfectly as soon as it comes to rest on the fronds of a lichen. Another well-known bark-living spider is *Drapetisca socialis*, which also avoids predators by having cryptic colouration against a lichen background. Living within the leafy growth of the larger lichens are spiders such as *Lathys humilis* and *Cryphoeca silvicola*, as well as many smaller animals which graze the lichens and algae.

Below: The lichen Parmelia caperata forms yellow-green rosettes with 'leafy' lobes on the bark of trees. It is widespread in northern Europe but is declining because of its sensitivity to aerial pollution.

NATIONAL PARKS AS SANCTUARIES

A great deal of wildlife has evolved in association with a natural forest cover and the best place to preserve it is in national parks and nature reserves. The earliest protected areas, however, were not created solely for wildlife; the world's first national park, Yellowstone, was set aside in 1872 as a wilderness area where man could find peace and contentment. This approach was copied in many other countries: 1887 saw the creation of the Banff National Park in the Canadian Rockies, and soon afterwards the idea spread to Europe where many wild and beautiful areas in the mountains became national parks. Although the number of parks and nature reserves now reaches many hundreds throughout Europe and North America, the bias is still heavily in favour of sites in mountainous areas, where agriculture is of little importance and there are few human settlements. This imbalance is probably true of most countries, particularly as lowland forests have already been cleared or else are in commercial production. In Britain economic exploitation is not permitted on the National Nature Reserves, which are managed primarily for wildlife, but it has been difficult to give national parks this sort of protection. In the Canadian Banff National Park coal mining and lumbering continued for a long period after the establishment of the park, and the former did not cease until 1923 – thirty-six years later.

In the Pyrenees the Spanish Aigues Tortes National Park has been completely altered in character by the construction of hydroelectric works, while in most French national parks timber exploitation continues even today. Foresters claim that selective felling would be permitted in the park forests because the total area of woodland is not reduced. However, we have already seen how noisy silvicultural operations such as the use of machines, road-building and so on cause the rare European brown bear to abandon its territory. The harvesting of mature wood also means that old half-rotten trees, which provide a nesting or feeding habitat for many wild creatures and which would be widespread in a natural forest, become very scarce.

The number of people who visit the parks has increased enormously in recent times and many conservationists now feel that too much emphasis has been placed on their role as places for public enjoyment. In 1965 it was estimated that 120 million people visited the national and provincial parks in North America and it is predicted that this total will rise to about 330 million by the end of the century. Unfortunately even the most considerate visitors can cause physical damage by repeated trampling, resulting in path erosion, destruction of the vegetation cover and disturbance. In addition, as visitors increase in number, so the demand for roads, hostels, hotels, car-parking facilities, camp sites, ski-lifts and

Above: Ordesa National Park in the Spanish Pyrenees occupies a steep-sided mountain valley with some spectacular scenery. There are forests of beech, pine and oak with the shrubby mountain pine at the higher levels.

Previous page: Peyto Lake in the Banff National Park. This park is considered by many to have the most beautiful scenery in all of Canada's lake-strewn landscape.

ki-runs also increases. The original commercial exploitation by mining and lumbering has declined as a result of enlightened land management, but the impact of large numbers of tourists is in turn bringing its own problems. Many of the North American parks have adopted a zoning system whereby a small area is set aside for car parks, camp sites, picnic areas and other facilities but the rest of the park is left undisturbed. This system works well until the number of visitors increases to a level which demands a further expansion of the tourist facilities. Eventually some limitation on access will be necessary in order to maintain the unspoilt nature of the forests and to keep disturbance to a minimum.

In North America, Japan and some other countries, most of the land in national parks is owned by the state, allowing a large measure of protection by government action. Elsewhere there may be considerable problems in establishing effective park management. In Britain the land in national parks is privately owned and the Park Authority has limited powers. In France the central government provides the funds but most of the land is owned by the communes, whose representatives may dominate the Park Authority. This can lead to an unusual situation where exploitation of the forest and hunting continue because these rights have been traditionally held by the local people and the state has little power to intervene. A similar situation is found in national

parks in Spain, where uncontrolled grazing may be the greatest problem.

France has adopted a zoning system to separate different types of use but it is quite unlike the American concept. There is a central region usually consisting of the highest sections of the park, where control may be very effective. Development work such as roads, building and camp sites is not permitted. This central zone is the park proper and is managed by a Council of Administration through a director and staff. Around the park is a peripheral zone, generally larger in area and entirely controlled by the departmental authority, where all sorts of tourist developments are permitted and even encouraged by financial support from the central government. The danger of this system is that in the long run the smaller inner zone will become encircled by a concentration of recreational facilities which in many cases could be detrimental to the preservation of wildlife within the park proper. Perhaps one of the factors contributing to this problem is that the concept of management for wildlife (as opposed to game) within forests in national parks and nature reserves is not very well developed in many parts of the world. Advice on management is usually provided by the forest service, but as its staff are trained primarily in timber exploitation and game management the principles of ecological management for wildlife are seldom properly understood. Fortunately this situation is

Above: The Abruzzo National Park of Italy protects a small herd of a unique race of chamois quite distinct from the typical race found in the Alps.

113

gradually improving due to public opinion and the wealth of conservation literature now available.

There are some notable exceptions to the commercial approach to forest management in national parks; two are worth special mention. The beautiful Swiss National Park in the Engadine, created in 1914, now covers 17,000 hectares, including 5,000 hectares of forest. The more accessible parts of the forest suffered severely before 1914 as a great deal of timber was cut for charcoal production and the presence of iron-ore and silver-bearing lead mines resulted in the construction of smelting works, which also made demands on timber resources. These activities ceased many years ago and the forests have regenerated naturally. In 1914 the wilderness concept was very much in the minds of the founders of the park and at that time tourism was not a problem. The purpose of the park is stated in the Swiss law as 'an alpine sanctuary protected from all human interference and influences not serving its purpose and where the entire fauna and flora are allowed to develop freely'. The park regulations forbid shooting, fishing, camping, lighting fires, the collection or killing of any animals, birds or plants, and the cutting of wood. No grazing is permitted and no dogs may be taken into the park even if on a leash. Visitors who break the regulations are liable to a fine of 500 francs (£125 or $243). This comprehensive protection was quite unusual for the time and the park is an outstanding example of a protected area, even though the numbers of tourists have multiplied tenfold in the last decade and the park authorities find it increasingly difficult to resist the pressures for more roads, car-parks and access routes.

The Swiss National Park began with clearly stated objectives and firm control, but this was not the case with the Abruzzo National Park in the central Apennines of Italy. Situated not far from Rome and

Right: The wood anemone carpets the ground with its white o pinkish flowers in the spring and early summer before the leaves of the tree canopy have grown to obscure the sunshine.

Below: Bluebells thriv best in the moist Atlantic climate of Britain but also occur in western parts of the European continent.

Naples, the park was established in 1923 and gradually extended from the original 18,000 hectares to the 30,000 hectares it is today. The land is controlled by a Park Authority but is privately owned and restrictions on exploitation were much resented and generally ignored. Winter resorts were built, large areas of woodland were cleared for ski-runs, roads, as well as the construction of many private villas. In 1964 a committee of the International Union for the Conservation of Nature expressed alarm at these events. Since then enormous improvement has been made due to the enlightened approach of the present director. Much of the exploitation has been stopped, the park pays rent for the best woodland in order to preserve the trees, and compensation is paid to local farmers and shepherds for damage caused by bears and wolves, even if this takes place outside the park boundaries. The strong opposition to the park by people living in the area has changed to one of tolerance or even pride in the part they can play in maintaining this marvellous piece of Italian heritage.

The success of park management therefore depends on getting the co-operation and understanding of the local people and visiting public, and a great deal of educational work is needed before this can be achieved. Unfortunately there are still too many examples of parks where little attempt has been made to do this. The magnificent Covadonga National Park in the Cantabrian mountains has some of the loveliest scenery in northern Spain and is a popular tourist area. The difficulties of management stem from the fact that nearly all the land is privately owned and a very small proportion is state-controlled. The traditional grazing by sheep, goats, cattle and horses continues without restriction and the poor condition of the vegetation in many areas suggests that the stocking rate is too high. Timber exploitation is permitted. Mining for iron and manganese ores was licensed in 1940, not ceasing until 1972 when all profitable seams had been worked out. Meanwhile public use is increasing rapidly with virtually no restrictions on what visitors are allowed to do.

In eastern Europe there are fewer complications over national park management because the state controls the land. The Tatra National Park, in the Carpathians, partly in Poland and partly in Czechoslovakia, is a splendid region of forest, mountain and lakes. Visitors are expected to keep to the footpaths which are well signposted and to ski-runs in areas where winter sports are allowed. No domestic grazing is permitted and an area of 9,940 hectares has been set aside as a strict reserve which the public must not enter. Although there are relatively few restrictions on recreational use, freedom from commercial exploitation must reduce the disturbance to the forest wildlife.

Management for conservation of natural forest and its wildlife requires only protection from disturbance and freedom from exploitation but, where the woodland has been exploited, active restoration may be necessary over a period of many years. For example, in the Spanish Pyrenees the old beech forests that were formerly very widespread have been fragmented or destroyed in many areas by intensive sheep and goat grazing which prevents regeneration. In some regions beech forest has been fenced in order to keep out stock and young trees soon appear around the parent plants. Silvicultural management over many centuries not only alters the structure of the woodland and the tree species present but also determines the wildlife which will survive.

In modern times new uses for trees are being found. In low rainfall areas shelter-belts slow down the wind velocity, reduce evaporation from the soil and prevent dust-storms. Trees stabilize sand dunes along many coastlines and are particularly important on the Atlantic coast of France and in western Jutland, Denmark. In European Russia, extensive areas of moving sands have been stabilized by tree planting, while forest belts along roads and railways passing through desert country protect traffic from sand-drifts and winter snow. Trees are also important in the restoration of industrial wasteland and mining spoil heaps. After such land has been shaped to fit the contours of the surrounding countryside, quick-growing trees are planted; as they grow they provide a local amenity as well as a habitat for wildlife.

Although natural forest is becoming increasingly rare in many parts of the world, there is now a greater understanding of the important rôle which trees, as individuals and as a forest environment, have in the affairs of man. We must improve on this knowledge and look, in the words of one of Britain's leading ecologists, Charles Elton, 'for some wise principle of co-existence between man and nature, even if it has to be a modified kind of man and a modified kind of nature.'

Left: The Covadonga National Park in the Cantabrian mountains of northern Spain is often shrouded in mist as moist air from the Bay of Biscay is cooled on the mountain slopes. While the climate is excellent for tree growth, this is prevented by intensive grazing.

Right: The High Tatra National Park lies partly in Czechoslovakia and partly in Poland. This view shows the Lomnický štít in Czechoslovakia

ACKNOWLEDGMENTS

Heather Angel: 4/5, 7, 38, 40 Bottom, 43; G. Bernard/Jacana: 25 Bottom; Dr. L. Boitani: 80; A. & E. Bomford/Ardea Photographics: 44; J. D. Bradley/Natural Science Photos: 50; W. Brooks/Bruce Coleman: 36/37, 98/99; J. Brun/Jacana: 8, 93; B. & C. Calhoun/Bruce Coleman: 35; G. Churchouse: 42; C. T. K. Czechoslovakia: 117; A. Davies: 9, 56, 57, 95, 108, 109; C. De Klemm/Jacana: 30; A. Ducrot/Jacana: 67, 70 Bottom; E. Duffey: 28, 29, 33, 83, 112, 113, 114, 116; R. Fletcher: 16/17, 48/49, 62/63; J. Foott/Bruce Coleman: 79 Bottom, 84; Werner Forman Archive: 11; N. Fox-Davies/Bruce Coleman: 16 Top Left; S. Gooders/Ardea Photographics: 115; J. A. Grant: 60, 61; K. Gunnar/Bruce Coleman: 97 Top, 110/111; B. Hawkes/Jacana: 54 Bottom; J. P. Hervy/Jacana: 55 Bottom; IGDA/Archive B: 12, 14; IGDA/C. Bevilacqua: 49 Right; IGDA/Gogna & Machetto: 20; IGDA/Pajsajes Espanoles: 107; IGDA/M. Pedone: 19, 26/27, 106; IGDA/P. 2.: 31; IGDA/C. Sappa: 25 Top; IGDA/J. M. Steinlein: 26; IGDA/A. Vergani: 91; E. Kroll/Taurus Photo: 102; G. Langsbury/Bruce Coleman: 92; A. P. Layman: 32; A. Leinonen/Bruce Coleman: 73; J-C. Maes/Jacana: 68, 74; Magnus/Jacana: 85; J. Markham/Bruce Coleman: 66; W. Mason: 24, 54 Top; J. L. Mason: 51 Centre, 52, 53; J. Massey Stewart: 22; M. R. Mitchell: 55 Top; C. & M. Moiton/Jacana: 97 Bottom; N. Myers/Bruce Coleman: 105 Right; C. Ott/Bruce Coleman: 64, 86, 101 Top Right; A. Owczarzak/Taurus Photo: 103; Oxford Scientific Films: 58/59; C. N. Page: 23; Dr. L. Pellegrini: 40 Top; A. Pitcairn/Grant Heilman: 13; W. Ratcliffe: 37 Right, 39; H. Reinhard/Bruce Coleman: 100/101; G. R. Roberts: 41, 104/105; S. Roberts/Ardea Photographics: 69; L. L. Rue III/Bruce Coleman: 18, 72, 79 Top, 90, 94/95, 98 Bottom; C. E. Schmidt/Taurus Photo: 70 Top; N. Tomalin/Bruce Coleman: 6; United States National Park Service/Photo-M. Woodbridge Williams: Title Page, Half Title Page; J. Van Wormer/Bruce Coleman: 75, 87; P. Varin/Jacana: 81; Varin-Visage/Jacana: 65, 76, 78, 88, 96; H. Veiller/Jacana: 45; R. Volot/Jacana: 71; P. Ward: 48 Top; P. Ward/Natural Science Photos: 51; F. Winner/Jacana: 89.

METRIC-IMPERIAL CONVERSION TABLES

metres	feet	hectares	acres	°C	°F		
1	3.3	1	2·5	−50	−58	1 mm	= 0.039 inches
5	16.4	5	12.4	−40	−40	1 cm	= 0.39 inches
20	32.8	10	24.7	−30	−22	1 km	= 0.62 mile
25	82	50	124	−20	−4	1 tonne	= 0.98 UK tons
50	164	100	247	−10	14	1 tonne	= 1.10 short (US) tons
75	246	200	494	−5	23	1 litre	= 0.22 UK gallons
100	328	300	741	0	32	1 litre	= 0.26 US gallons
200	656	400	988	5	41		
300	984	500	1235	10	50		
400	1312	600	1482	20	68		
500	1640	700	1730	30	86		
600	1968	800	1977	40	104		
700	2296	1000	2471	50	122		
800	2624	2000	4942				
900	2952	5000	12,355				
1000	3280	20,000	24,710				
2000	3380						
2000	6560						
2500	8202						

NDEX

bruzzo National Park, 29, 82, **83**, 84, 85, **113**, 114–118
lder, 20, 21, 32
lpenrose, 15
mbrosia beetles, 57
neurophyton, 13
pple, 23
raucariaceae, 40
rbutus, 26
rchaeopteris, 13
sh, 38, 91
   European, 23
   flowering, 39
spen, 15, 20, 21
zalea,
   Pontic, 22

adgers, 46, 95, **95**
ald eagle, 75, 76
amboo,
   Kuril, 22
anff National Park, 87, 112
arbery, 23
ark and wood eaters,
   ambrosia beetles, 57
   bark beetles, 57–58
asswood, 37
ats, 46, 79
ay, red, 34
ayheads, 34
ear,
   black, (*See* Black bears)
   brown, (*See* Brown bears)
   grizzly, **85**, **86**, 86–87
eavers, **97**, **98**, **99**
   decline of, 96
   protection of, 98
   re-introduction of, 97
eech, **7**, 15, **17**, 20, 26, 28, 29, 31, 37, 46, 62, **63**, 91
   black, 42
   fauna, 46
   hard, 42
   mountain, 42
   Nothofagus, 40, 42
   red, 42
   silver, 42
eech-fir, 33
ialowieza National Park, 32–33
ilberry, 21
irch, 20, 21, 23, 39, 75, 109
   conditions for, 8
   Erman's, 22
   Karelian, 21
   yellow, 37
irds,
   coniferous forests, in, 66
   counterparts in different
      continents, 71, 74–75
   feeding habits of, 66–67
   prey, of, 72–78
   temperate forests, in, 65
lack bears, 87, **87**
ox, 28
roadleaved woodlands, 23
room, common, 15
romeliads, 34

Brown bears,
   breeding habits, 85
   decline of, 46, 82–83
   hibernation of, 84–85
   predators, 85
   protection of, 83, 84
Brown creepers, 71
Buzzards, 72

Calasoma,
– *C. inquisitor*, 53
– *C. sycophanta*, 53
Caribou, 92
Cats, wild, 46, 79, 100
Cedar, 20, 21, 84
   Algerian, 30
   Atlas, 30
   Korean, 23
   Lebanon, of, **30**, 30
   western red, 39
   white, 37
Chaffinches, 46, 67
Chamise, 34
Chaparral, 34
Cherry,
   black, 37
Chestnut, 26, 28
   horse, 31
   sweet, 25, 28
Chickadees, 71
Cicadas, **60**, **61**, 61
Coal, 13–14
Conifers,
   deciduous trees, and, 28
   early, 14
   extent of, 15, 16, 28
   temperature and, 15, 18
   wintering in, 15
Coppice,
   meaning of, 20
Covadonga National Park, **29**, 116, **116**
Cork,
   Amur, 23
   oak, 25, 26–27, 30, 31
Cougars, 79
Cowberry, 21
Coyote, 81
Crab spider, 109
Cranberry, 15
Crossbills, 65, 68
Cryphoeca silvicola, 109
Cypress, 34

Darwin, Charles, 39
Decay, 62–63
Deciduous trees,
   conifers, and, 18
   extent of, 15–16
   leaf-fall in, 15
   temperature and, 15, 18
   water loss in, 15
   wintering in, 15
Deer,
   Chinese water, 92
   fallow, 92, **93**
   red, **8**, **88**, **89**, 89, 90
   roe, 91–92, **92**
   tree damage by, 91
Deforestation,

America, in, 8, 20
   axe, by, 8–9
   early, 68
   Eastern Europe, in, 32–33
   Europe, in, 9, 10
   fuel-collecting, by, 33
   generally, 103
   grazing, by, 31
   Mediterranean, 26, 31
   Middle East, 8
   natural disaster, by, 33
   New Zealand, in, 42
   'slash and burn', by, 9
   Western Europe, in, 23
Drapetisca socialis, 109
Draved forest, 8
Dutch elm disease, **56**, **57**, 58

Ecosystem,
   meaning of, 45
Elk, 89
Elm, 21, 23, 38
Elton, Charles, 117
Everglades National Park, 34–37

Fabre, Jean Henri, 55–56
Falcons, 72
Fir, 20, 28, 75
   alpine, 39
   douglas, 39
   Manchurian, 23
   Sakhalin, 22
   silver, 26, **37**, 39
Firecrest, 71
Flint tools, 9
Foliage feeders, 50–51, 52
Forests (*see also* Silviculture)
   air pollution and, 108, 109
   boundaries, 9, 10
   Chile, in, 39–40
   clearings, cultivation of, 8, 9, 10
   cultivated, 25
   conservation of, 104–107
   Eastern Europe, in, 32–33
   exploitation of, (*see also* Timber)
      10
   extent of, 7, 15
   fires, 10, 34
   food supply, as, 7
   mammals of the, 79–109
   Mediterranean, 26
   Magellanic, 40
   Neolithic period, in, 8, 9
   New Zealand, in, 40–43
   North Africa, in, 30–31, 34–39
   pests, (*See* Forest pests)
   reverence for, 7–8
   Southern Hemisphere, in, 39–43
   steppes, 23
   USSR, in, 20–23
   Valdivian, 39–40
   Western Europe, in, 25
Forest pests,
   pine looper moths, 56
   pine processionary, 55–56
   pine sawfly, 56
   wood wasps, 58
Formica rufa, 53–54
Foxes, **94**, 94–95
Fur-bearing animals, 96

Galls, 51–52
Garigue, 26
Genet, 79, 100–101
Goldcrest, 66, 71
Golden-crowned kinglet, 71
Golden eagle, 75
Gorse, 15
Goshawks, 72, **73**, 74
   American, 74–75
Gran Paradiso, 29–30
Grape,
   Amur, 23
Grimes Graves, 9
Gumbo limbo, 34

'Halny', the, 33
Hammocks, 34
Harvestmen, 54
Hawks, 72
Hayley Wood, 9, 10
Hazel, 23
Hemlock,
   eastern, 16, 37
   western, **37**, 39
Holly, 15, 34
Holm oak, 26, 38
Hooker, Joseph, 39
Hornbeam, **9**, 18, 23, 29, 32
   hop-, 29
Hunting, 10, 25
   North America, in, 89
   reserves, 29–30, 32, 33

Ichneumonid fly, 58–59, **59**
Ivy Subatlantic, 15

Jasmine, 23
Jays, 46, 65
Juniper, 30
   Spanish, 28
Juniperus virginiana, 16

Kamahi, 42
Kauri, 40–42
Kishmish, 23
Kites, 72
Kohekohe, 42

Larch, 18, **19**, 20, 21, 29, 58
   Daurian, 22, 23
Lathys humilis, 109
Laurel, 40, 42
Leaf-miners, 52, 53
Lemons, 38
Lepidodendron, 14
Lichens, 108–109, **108**, **109**
Lime, 20, 21, 28, 32
   Amur, 23
   Manchurian, 23
   small-leaved, 23
Lynx, 79

Magnolia, 34, 40
   Chinese, 23
Mahogany,
   Madeira, 34
Mangrove, 34–37
Maple, 23, 75
   Montpellier, 28, 30
   Norway, 23

sugar, 37
Maquis, 26
Martens, 46, 79, **100**
Matorral, 26, 27, 34
Miro, 42
Mixed forest belt, 23
Moose, 89, **90**
Moths, 46, **50**, **51**
  defoliators, as, 50–51
Mount Pindus nature reserve, **31**, 31
Mountain ash, 15
Muir, John, 107
Muntjac, 92
Myrtle, 42

National parks,
  generally, 112–117
Nothofagus, 40, 42, **43**
Nutcrackers, 65, **67**, 68
  thick-billed, 66–67

Oak, 15, 18, 20, 23, 26, 28, 32, 34,
  37, **45**, **48**, 75, 91, 109
  -apple, 51
  bog, 49
  cork, 25, **26**, 26–27, 30, 31
  distribution of, 45
  downy, 29
  evergreen, 26, 30, 31
  fauna, 49
  galls, **51**, **52**, 51–52
  Gambel, 34
  holm, 26, 38
  importance of, 45–48
  kermes, 26
  Lusitanian, 28
  Magnolian, 23
  pedunculate, 23, 28
  predators of, 50–53
  Pyrenean, 28
  scrub, 34
  sessile, 28, 29
  turkey, 29
  white, 28
Olives, **27**, 27, 28
Oranges, 28
Osprey, **75**, 75–76
Owls,
  barn, 76–78
  eagle, 46, 76–78, **77**
  generally, 72
  great grey, 76
  pigmy, 76
  tawny, 76, 78

Palm, 34
  date-, 28
  dwarf, 26
  royal, 34
Pear, 23
Pepper, wild, 23
Philodromus emerginatus, 109
Picea,
  – *P. abies*, 18
  – *P. obavata*, 18
Pine, 20, 26, 28, 31, 32, 91, 109
  Aleppo, 27, 30, 31
  bristle-cone, 39, 64
  conditions for, 16–18
  dwarf mountain, 20

jack, 37
Japanese stone, 21, 22
-looper moth, 56
maritime, 25, 27, 30
Monterey, 42
mountain, 29
ponderosa, 39
processionary, **55**, 55–56
red, 37
sawfly, 56
Scots, 23, **44**, 58
stone, 30, 67
sugar, 39
Weymouth, 16
white, 37
white-barked, 39
Pinelands, 34–37
Pine marten, 96, 100
Pinus,
– *P. radiata*, 42, 43
– *P. strobus*, 16
– *P. sylvestris*, 18
Podocarps, 40, 40, 42
Polecat, 100
Pollen,
  archeological source, as, 8–10
Pollution,
  air, 108, 109
  New Zealand paper industry,
    from, 43
  Swedish timber industry, from,
    43
Poplar, 20, 75, 91, **106**
  yellow, 37
Porcupines, 79

Quercus, 30
– *Q. petrea*, 45
– *Q. robur*, 45
– *Q. rotundifolia*, 26

Rabbits, 94
Racoons, 79
Rata, 42
Red-breasted nuthatches, 71
Redstarts, 65
Redwood, **6**, **39**, 68
Reindeer, **91**, 92
Rimu, 42
Roosevelt, Theodore, 204
Rosalia alpina, 46
Ruby-crowned kinglet, 71
Russian forests, (*see also* Taiga)
  trees of, 20, 21

Sagebrush,
  Great Basin, 34
Sapsuckers, 68–69, **69**
Scolytidae, 57
Sequoia
– *S. gigantea*, **6**, **39**, 39, **105**, 106
– *S. sempervirens*, 106
Sika, 92
Silviculture,
  general, 25
  water quality, effect of, 107–108
Sparrowhawks, 46, 72–74, **74**
Spiders, 54
Spindle, 23

Spruce, 18, 20, 23, **24**, 29, 33, 58,
  75, 91
  Engelmann, 39
  Jeddo, 21, 22
  sitka, 39
Squirrels, 46, 79, 101, **101**
Standards,
  meaning of, 20
Strawberry tree, 28
Subor, 18
Swiss National Park, 67, 114
Sycamore, 28, 49

Taiga,
  generally, 20–21
  subzones of, 21–22
  trees of, 21, **22**
Taraire, 42
Tatra National Park, 33, 82, 116
Tetraxylopteris, 13
Timber,
  cropping of, 10
  generally, 57
  production of, 25
Titmice, 65, 71
Tits, 65, **66**, 67, 71
Tortes National Park, 112
Totara, 42
Towaii, 42
Treecreepers, 65, 71–72
Trees,
  ancient religion, in, 7–8
  attack by man on, 68
  Carboniferous period, in, 13–14
  dead or dying, as habitat, 62–63
  Cretaceous period, in, 15
  deciduous (*see* Deciduous trees)
  Devonian period, in, 13, 14
  Eocene period, in, 10
  fossil, 13
  Mesozoic period, in, 14
  Permian period, in, 14
Truffles, 25
Tsuga canadensis, 16

Ursus horribilis, 86–87

Viburnum, 26
Victor Emanuel II, 39
Victor Emanuel III, 30
Vines, 38, 34
Voroniez National Park, 98

Walnut, 25
  Manchurian, 23
Wapiti, 89, 90–91
Warblers, 46, 66
Willows, 91
Wolf,
  cattle, as predator of, 81
  destruction of the, 79–81
  ecological factor, as, 82
  grey, 79–82, **81**
  protection of the, **80**, 82
  red, 82
  Spanish, 82
Wood ants, 53–54, **54**
Woodpeckers, 46, 65, 68, **68**, **70**
  greater spotted, 66
  three-toed, 71

Wood wasps, 58
  parasites of, 58–59
Wrens, 65

Yellowstone National Park, 86, 112
Yew, 28, 29
  acutifoliate, 23